LIVING WITH
NO EXCUSES

—

LIVING WITH
NO EXCUSES

The Remarkable Rebirth
of an American Soldier

Noah Galloway

with Rebecca Angel Baer

CENTER
STREET®

NEW YORK   BOSTON   NASHVILLE

Center Street
Hachette Book Group
1290 Avenue of the Americas, New York, NY 10104
centerstreet.com
twitter.com/centerstreet

First Edition: August 2016

Center Street is a division of Hachette Book Group, Inc. The Center Street name and logo are trademarks of Hachette Book Group, Inc.

The publisher is not responsible for websites (or their content) that are not owned by the publisher.

The Hachette Speakers Bureau provides a wide range of authors for speaking events. To find out more, go to www.HachetteSpeakersBureau.com or call (866) 376-6591.

Title page image by Jason Maris.

Print book interior design by Timothy Shaner, nightanddaydesign.biz

ISBNs: 978-1-4555-9693-5 (hardcover), 978-1-4555-9692-8 (ebook)

Printed in the United States of America

RRD-C

10 9 8 7 6 5 4 3 2 1

FOR COLSTON, JACK, AND RIAN,
MY CHILDREN, WHO ARE
THE CENTER OF MY UNIVERSE.

CONTENTS

CONTENTS

LIVING WITH
NO EXCUSES

PART ONE
SURVIVAL

———

CHAPTER 1

Alive

(December 2005)

"THESE BOMBS are so hot that your bones will actually fuse together," someone said. I couldn't make out who said it, but at least I thought I heard it. I couldn't open my mouth. Panic surged through my body, as I feared my jaw was fused shut from an explosion. I tried and tried to open my mouth. And then I felt someone place an object in my hand and I heard, "If you're in pain, press this button."

My eyes popped open. It was a nightmare. Just a bad dream. But as my eyes darted around the room I suddenly realized I didn't know where I was. Gone was the hot desert sun, the swirling mix of dirt and sand, and comrades all around in camo. The sounds of war had been replaced with the faint sound of children's voices singing Christmas carols. Suddenly I was aware of severe pain that pulsed throughout every inch of my body. I remembered the device in my hand—I assumed it was a morphine drip. I pressed the button over and over again, but there was no relief from the unbearable pain.

Then the door to the room swung open. In walked a man, a nurse, looking really annoyed.

"We've got kids out here singing Christmas carols for us because we're away from our families and you're being rude," he said. Turns out I'd moved my finger from the morphine button to the nurse's call button.

Are you kidding me? I thought. I couldn't respond because I couldn't open my mouth. He knew that as he stood there smugly. I glared back at him and saw his name on the plastic tag attached to the pocket on his scrubs. I can't remember his name now, but at the time I repeated his name over and over again in my head. I let the pain engulf me as his name became a steady beat like a drum, and the angry rhythm in my head lulled me back to a deep, drugged sleep.

When I came to again the nurse was gone. My focus was hazy at best but in his place I saw a doctor and I heard him say, "I'll take care of this one." And he stayed with me until three flight nurses arrived in Air Force uniforms. I remember the uniforms and I remember how nice they were to me. I was carefully moved from my bed to a gurney and wheeled outside and onto an ambulance truck. The frosty December air hit my body with a shock and I shivered. I remember the bitterness of the cold. It was December in Germany and my body hadn't adjusted from the oppressive heat of the war zone. As the gurney was rolled toward the ambulance I heard another man shouting and ranting. He was a frail, elderly black man and he was screaming words that didn't make sense. I looked up to the flight nurses to ask with my eyes, "What is wrong with him?" One of the nurses answered me saying that he was a veteran who had remained in Germany after completing his service. He was dying. They were taking him home so he could die surrounded by his loved ones. As I tried to make out what he was trying to say I found myself distracted, even just momentarily, from my pain and my confusion. I still didn't really know why I was there or what had happened. But I looked up at the kind faces of the three nurses and felt comforted.

When the ambulance reached the end of the runway, both the dying man and I were transferred onto the plane. Instead of the small seats you'd find crammed together in a commercial plane, there were beds attached parallel to the wall. I was carefully placed on one. The nurses did everything they could to make me comfortable. When I was settled in, ready to go home, I finally felt warmth—whether from the blankets or the compassion, it didn't matter. I was cared for throughout the entire flight and then after a long time one of the nurses leaned down to me and said, "We'll be landing soon, so you'll wake up in the hospital." He gave me a shot and I was out.

I woke up in a tiny hospital room. I didn't know where yet, but I saw the brightness of the fluorescent light streaming in from the hallway as the door opened slowly. I blinked as figures came into focus. I saw her first: petite frame, curly white hair, and glasses. It was my mom! My mom and dad were in the room. I was somewhere safe.

They were smiling, but I could see they were scared. And my immediate thought was, *Smile so they know you are okay.* I learned later that because my family had missed one of their flights, they arrived after midnight and there was no one to prepare them for what they would see, or tell them about the condition I was in.

The next few days are a painful, terrifying blur. One minute I would be sweating, the next freezing. I was either in pain or I was passed out. In the blink of an eye, I had gone from a fearless, strong soldier fighting a war to feeling like a helpless child. I had no idea how to react to where I was or what was happening to me. One minute I was angry and the next I was overcome with emotion and crying. I cried a lot. I have never been so scared.

Those first few days in Walter Reed Army Medical Center, in Washington, D.C., were more terrifying than anything I encountered in Iraq. Each time I was deployed I had accepted that I could die. I prepared myself to die in Iraq. It never crossed my mind that I could wake up in a hospital bed severely injured. We had already lost some of the guys in my company. They weren't injured, they were killed, and we had all accepted that risk. It wasn't supposed to go this way. I wasn't supposed to be writhing in pain in a hospital room in Washington, D.C. I was supposed to be still in Iraq or dead. There was no in between. I didn't know how to handle in between.

My fear was amplified each time I was taken out of that stiflingly small hospital room, because every time they came to get me, I was wheeled into another painful surgery. I was heavily medicated but that only took the edge off the pain and added to my confusion. I still didn't really know what was going on or what had happened to me. And now I was in and out of consciousness, so I couldn't get a firm grasp on reality. At one point on one of these trips to surgery, I remember grabbing my mom's arm. I clutched on to her and begged her, "Don't let them take me, please don't let them take me again."

When there was a lull in the trips to the operating room my mom was the one who finally told me the extent of my injuries. My mom is a very sweet, unassuming person, but she's also very direct. There would be no sugarcoating here. She was working hard to be strong for me and I remember her walking into the room normally, as if everything were fine, and standing by my bed as she rattled off my injuries in a very matter-of-fact fashion—as if she were listing the ingredients in a recipe. "You lost your left arm above the elbow, your left leg above the knee, you have severe injuries to your right leg, your right hand also sustained some injuries, and your jaw is wired shut."

My mom was far better at masking her emotions than my dad was. He was standing behind her as she told me, but he never said a word. This was a lot for Dad to take in. He lost his arm at age eighteen in an industrial accident. All I'd ever known was a dad with one arm. As I sat there stunned, processing all Mom had just told me, she filled the silence in the room with, "Look, this is what it is and now let's figure out what's next."

My next reaction was, "Who died?" Because if I was that bad off, then how was everyone else? It wasn't until about a week later that I received a call from my platoon leader telling me that I took the worst of it. There were only three of us in the vehicle that night and I was the most severely injured. So, with the knowledge that everyone else was going to be okay, my attention turned to what I was going to do.

I had always been a very physically active person. And I loved my job. I got into the military because of September 11, but I stumbled into a career that I absolutely loved. I was meant to be an infantry soldier. I thought, *I will never be physical again and my career in the military is over.* One tiny trip wire had taken everything away from me in one explosive moment.

I sank into a very dark place. I wallowed in both my physical pain and my mental anguish. One day my parents were sitting by my side in the hospital room—as they did every day—and I turned to my mom and blurted out, "How am I ever gonna be able to tie my shoes again?"

Mom rebutted my pity party with, "Well, your father can tie his shoes with one hand. Andy! Show Noah how you can tie your shoes with one hand." And as I started to protest, Dad cut my whining off at the pass. "Oh my gosh, Noah, I can tie my shoes with one hand." And he did, as I had seen him do so many times growing up. "I just need a little sympathy," I said. To which Mom replied, "Well, you're not getting it today."

A few days after I'd had my shoelace meltdown, after many tears, I found myself drained of emotion, a hollowed-out shell. My mother saw the blank expression on my face and she saw an opportunity to drag me out of the fog. She took it. She came up to my bed, leaned in close—but not so close that the other people in the room couldn't hear her, and said, "You just had to outdo your dad and lose your arm and your leg." She smiled, waiting for my reply, but all I could do was laugh. It was funny but it was also at that moment that I think I felt a little spark of excitement and anticipation again. It would take a while to fully ignite the flame but what she said definitely tapped into some important part of me. I have a very competitive side and Mom knew that. She knew just what to say to shake me up, so I could realize, *Okay, life will go on from here.* I thought to myself, *My dad could do a whole lot with just one hand. Imagine how much more impressive it'll look with two missing limbs.* And I smiled the best I could through a wired jaw.

CHAPTER 2

Harsh Realities

(December 2005–January 2006)

I SPENT MUCH of those first few weeks in a drugged haze. I was in and out of the present. On one of my trips outside of my head and outside of that tiny hospital room, I found myself back in the sweaty, gritty desert I'd left so abruptly.

*   *   *

My unit was deep in a perilous region of Iraq. We lived among the enemies we were fighting, even though we frequently didn't even know who they were. We were far away from the comforts other soldiers found in camp. We didn't have access to phones and it was a month before I was able to call home for the first time. After that, I managed to call home only every couple of weeks at best. Our missions kept us far removed from the realities of everyday life back home. At that point though I only wanted to know how my son, Colston, was doing. Brandi and I really had nothing to say to one another. Our relationship was deeply fractured before I left. I had little hope it would ever be repaired. I hadn't pulled the trigger on divorce, but I had actively thought about it. I saw a lawyer. I just didn't make my move. I only got so far as to transfer my power of attorney to my mother.

On one call I remember Brandi's voice sounded so chipper when she picked up the phone. I could almost see her smiling as she answered, but as soon as she heard my voice on the other end of the line, her tone immediately changed. Everything she said after that was in a monotone. She had no emotion left for me.

"Hey, what's going on?" I asked.

"I just can't do it anymore. You obviously love the Army more than me. We're not happy. I can't do it anymore," she repeated.

"I understand. It makes sense. When I get back, we'll finalize everything," I replied and hung up.

I felt like a rock had just sunk to the bottom of my stomach. We'd been in such bad shape for so long, but this was the end. She was right, of course. I did love this job more than I loved her. I had chosen the military over my marriage. I didn't mean to, but I had done exactly that.

I grabbed Jerry, my platoon leader, and stuttered, "Brandi and I are done."

Jerry pulled me away from the group behind the only cover available—a big mound of dirt. With his hand on my shoulder I sat there mumbling, "This sucks. I mean we're not in love, but it hurts." I told him how I'd already gone to a lawyer, that I knew we would be divorced when I got home, but the reality of it was unexpectedly overwhelming. I was so thankful to have Jerry there. By then we'd become fast friends, and out there, these guys were my family. We talked for a while and then I gave him a hug and thanked him. I took a deep breath and I was good to go. That was the last time I spoke to Brandi from Iraq.

*   *   *

When I lifted my heavy eyelids again, Brandi was standing there, clutching the side of my hospital bed. Her face was tear-stained, her eyes puffy and red from exhaustion. I reached up with my one hand and she tenderly took it in both of hers. She leaned in so she was closer to me. My mouth was still wired shut, so it was hard for me to get any words out. She leaned in and I said, "I know our marriage is over. But please just stay with me through this recovery." My eyes brimmed with tears, and fresh, salty drops were rolling down her face as she nodded yes.

What I didn't know was what had already been discussed before I even made it out of Germany. I had no idea what my family was going through back in Alabama or how they found out what had happened to me. I had no idea of the conversations they had until later. But when they were first notified I'd been injured, they assumed my condition was far less severe than it really was. I don't think my family ever really grasped that I could have been in that much danger. I never told them. On every call home, I made sure to make it sound like I wasn't doing anything near the fighting over there. I never wanted them to worry.

When the Army first notified my family, Brandi took Colston to my parents' house to wait for further instructions. She was pacing a lot and went outside for a cigarette. My dad joined her and asked her what was wrong.

"I don't know what to do. Noah and I have been talking about divorce. We were planning on getting a divorce," she said.

"What's going on out here?" my mom asked, as she came outside to join them.

"Brandi says she doesn't know what to do. She and Noah are getting divorced," Dad told Mom.

And my no-nonsense mother turned to Brandi and said, "You can go on home then. I'm gonna take care of my boy. He's going to be just fine. You can go now."

She meant what she said. Mom always does. But Brandi did come with my parents. She did stay once I asked her to, but it wasn't more than a week before I think she realized there wasn't really anything she could do. She wasn't needed. I was in and out of it, my mom and dad were there, and my sisters were on their way.

Mom pulled Brandi aside and said, "You can go home. Take care of Colston. Noah will be okay." So she left. As she walked out of the hospital, my three loving, overly protective, and, if I'm being honest, slightly intimidating sisters walked in the door. Jennifer told me later that as she, Katherine, and Sara marched into that hospital as Mom's reinforcements, they didn't utter a single word to Brandi. I knew what really happened between Brandi and myself, but to my sisters she was leaving me and they didn't owe her a thing. I believe in basketball it's called the "elbows out" approach. They didn't need to say a word to let anyone know that the Galloway women were taking charge now. Brandi was no longer needed to help their brother.

I understood why she left. I understood why our marriage failed. But Brandi's departure was when reality hit me like a wrecking ball. I no longer had anyone to worry about but myself. I had to face the facts. I remember thinking, *I've lost my job, two limbs, my wife, and everything I've known, and I'd rather be dead.*

My emotions were all over the map, though. I went from "This ain't nothing, I ain't worried about it. I'll make something of this," to "Why did this happen to me?" to crying like a baby, all in under a minute. But mostly everything was terrifying.

I was still in and out of consciousness so much, and so emotional. But there were little things that helped. I remember at one point hearing my dad say, "He likes music. I am going to put on some music." He brought in a little red radio and left it on this Top 40 station all the time hoping to cheer me up. Top 40 stations play the same songs over and over again. At the time there was one song that stood out and struck a chord with me: Sheryl Crow's "Good Is Good." I don't know what Sheryl Crow's intentions were when she wrote it, but I felt like she was singing to me directly.

I really related to this song. The words would bounce around my head even when I was asleep, about things going south and that it was up to you to make it better. Things are only as good as you make them. I felt calmer and comforted every time I heard it.

I was, however, still very much an emotional wreck and sometimes this resulted in misdirected anger. Unfortunately, my sisters bore the brunt of that. Sometimes I would just blow up without reason or warning. Once, my sister Sara was in the room and she was just moving things around, trying to clean up, and I blew up at her. She was so stunned and upset, she just walked out of the room and into the hallway to cry. Another soldier in a wheelchair came by and asked if she was okay. Through sobs and tears she choked out a "yeah."

"Did your soldier yell at you?" he asked. She nodded yes and he said, "I don't know why we do that. But don't take it personally. We're all going through it."

She calmed down and walked back in. She stood squarely in front of my bed and told me that I really pissed her off. Clearly I'd already forgotten I yelled at her because I looked at her with a bewildered expression and managed to push out through my wired jaw, "What's wrong with you?"

She glared at me and spat back, "You son of a bitch, you're what's wrong!" I was clueless. In fact, I pissed off my family members on a pretty regular basis until they figured out how to deal with it. They'd just control when I got to talk. My jaw was wired shut, but I could talk a little bit with some help.

I'd had a tracheotomy so I had a hole in my throat. I had this little purple plastic piece that I could put in the hole that would keep the air from coming out so I could talk. Every time I woke up, the purple plastic piece was clear across the room. They didn't keep it near me. I had to put my fingers over the hole so I could wheeze out, "Gimme...gimme...the...thing." I think this amused them.

After a while my dad grew concerned with how much medication I was being given. My dad formed this opinion based on his vast medical experience, having worked in construction. Obviously. But he harped on that topic a lot. It was his soapbox issue. Well, as it turned out, he was right.

I was being prepped for my umpteenth surgery and they injected me with the anesthetic. I was lying there waiting to fade out, waiting and waiting and waiting until they came to check on me, expecting to find me fast asleep. Instead, I was in that hospital bed, still totally awake. The nurses walked away but not far enough way so I missed what they said. I overheard one of the nurses say, "He's not going to sleep." Another said, "Well, he has so much medication in his system, it's probably not enough. He's going to have to go to surgery awake." I panicked and screamed, "NOOOOO! I'll go to sleep!" I closed my eyes and told myself, *Go to sleep, go to sleep, go to sleep.* Nothing happened. I did not go to sleep, so they took me into surgery awake. I was conscious but numb. I didn't feel physical pain, but I was completely freaked out.

Several more surgeries followed that one and with each one my terror only grew. I clung to my mother begging her to not let them take me. They started upping my dosage of medications because of all the anxiety. They were trying to calm me down. All along, Dad was standing there saying, "No. This is too much. This is too much."

Then late one night my dad's fears proved true. My blood pressure dropped dramatically, and I passed out. My parents called for help. A few of the nurses came in to try to wake me, but they couldn't. My parents stood in the corner of the room crying, thinking this was it. The doctors answered the page and got to work on me. An army of medical staff filled that tiny room working feverishly to save me, with the soundtrack of my parents' sobs in the background. Eventually they got my blood pressure back up and I was out of the woods. The very next morning the higher-ups from the hospital came down to apologize to my parents for what had happened. They assured my parents it wouldn't happen again. My dad said to them once again, this time a little more emphatically, "Y'all are medicating him too much." He wagged his finger, explaining to the doctors that

that was why I almost died. One of the doctors assured my dad he would take care of it.

They did lower the dosage of my medication, the benefit of which was that I was more lucid. The downside: I was now very aware of where I was. I was aware that I was in the hospital, missing two limbs, and terrified about the future.

CHAPTER 3

Uncle Johnny and the Open Door

(January 2006)

MY MOTHER'S BROTHER Johnny was a Vietnam vet, and he too had been wounded. He had spent a long time in a hospital and he understood more than most what I was going through. Or at least he thought he did, and I appreciated that— even if I didn't act like it at first. Uncle Johnny started to visit every weekend. He'd come and sit with me to give my parents a little breather.

After my dad won the battle over my medication, I was, as I said, a little more lucid. I was also a little more ornery. I wouldn't let anyone turn on that little red radio. I didn't even care if Sheryl Crow was telling me what was good. I was more aware of my pain. Just lying there and listening or doing anything at all hurt. My whole body hurt and everyone and everything was to blame. All I wanted to do was sit in silence with the door shut. Uncle

Johnny obliged me for a while. He'd come in and sit down in the chair next to my bed. He sat and stared blankly right along with me. But after a while, he couldn't handle that anymore.

One day, on the verge of dying of boredom, Uncle Johnny had had enough. He turned to me and said sternly, "Noah, I'm not gonna sit in here like we're in an oversized coffin. We're either opening the door or we're turning the TV on. Which one do you want?" I rolled my eyes and grumbled for a few minutes before answering, "All right. Turn on the TV." Without hesitation Uncle Johnny shot up out of that chair and reached up to hit the power button on the TV mounted from the ceiling. No sooner had his butt hit the chair seat than he was right back up again. "Fuck that. I am opening the door, too, because I want it open." He vigorously emphasized his intention so I didn't protest. He marched over and swung that door open. I swear he might have even taken a deep breath as if it were fresh mountain air. Then he came back to his chair and sat down.

There was a movie on starring Matthew Broderick. I'd never heard of it before but Uncle Johnny was explaining to me that this was a remake and Gene Wilder had played Broderick's character in the original film. In spite of myself, and my stubborn wish to sit and suffer in silence, I really liked the movie. And I remember thinking, *I am really enjoying myself.* I even turned to Uncle Johnny and said, "I'm glad we turned the TV on. This is great!" Uncle Johnny just smiled as if to say, "Of course! Finally!"

We were right in the middle of the movie when one of my machines started to malfunction. The machine's beeps drowned out the movie. A nurse came in to fix the problem and it just happened to be the hot nurse I had a crush on. She had short hair, a few tattoos on her arm, and she always wore a bandana over her head. The machine she was trying to fix was plugged in on the other side of the bed, up against the wall.

"Oh, I see. Hold on. I have to move the bed out from the wall to fix this," she said.

At this point I was just watching her. She fixed the machine and pushed the bed back up against the wall. She actually hit the wall with the bed and zap! The TV went out! "WHAT?! NO!" I screamed. She couldn't get it to turn back on. She tried but nothing worked.

"Oh no, I'm sorry. We'll have to get maintenance down here to fix it," she said with an apologetic look that I met with a glare of disdain. She was no longer hot to me. She was just the nurse who broke the TV. Maintenance didn't come to repair the TV until the next day. I didn't get to watch the rest of the movie. In fact, I never saw the end of the movie and I didn't even know the name of it until years later. Maybe one of these days I'll get to see *The Producers* from start to finish.

After the TV was fixed I stumbled across a show on the Discovery Channel, as I recall. It was about a guy who went into a jungle where no white man had gone before. He and his cameraman are told they will have to strip down to nothing before they can go any further and encounter the native population. They are then introduced to these tribesmen and are welcomed as members of the tribe. They get to know the tribesmen and experience their world. One of the things they experience is this tribe's puberty ritual, when a boy becomes a man. The boy goes into a little hut and takes some kind of drug. It's a mushroom or plant that they say hasn't made it to the white man's world yet. But in order to be accepted as a man in this tribe, you must first experience this drug. So the man goes into the hut and takes the drug. The camera is placed outside the hut. So you don't see him in there but you hear him moaning and then he's narrating what happened. And he says that every bad thing he had done in his life was haunting him while he was on this drug, even something as small as stealing a candy bar from a convenience store. Every relationship he's been in where he didn't treat a woman right tormented him. And you hear him in the hut moaning and crying and he says it was the most painful emotional experience he's ever had. At the end of the episode he comes out and he says he feels like the entire weight of the world has been lifted off him. He feels so good. And I remember watching it and thinking about it and comparing it to me being drugged up and having all of these emotions. Just days before I had been in and out of it and so emotional and scared and angry. I really related to this guy's experience.

Once Uncle Johnny forced me to turn the TV on I was reminded that there was life outside of that tiny room. There was so much more going on than just the pain, anger, and confusion I was feeling. And then he also opened the door. I was seeing people walking up and down the hallway. I was hearing other people's conversations. Uncle Johnny forced me to resume participation in life again by simply turning on the TV and opening the door.

CHAPTER 4

Turning Point

FROM THE BEGINNING of my time at Walter Reed I was in physical therapy. I hated it and never really wanted to go, but initially I had no choice. They wheeled my bed there. There's no escaping when you're immobile and basically a prisoner of your own bed.

One day about a month into my stay at Walter Reed they wheeled me down to a packed physical therapy room. There were other patients, wives, family members, and therapists filling the room almost to capacity. I was not thrilled to be there but was going through the exercises they were making me do, and then I looked up and saw Jennifer, Katherine, and Sara walk in pushing a stroller. Colston! My boy! The moment I saw him tears started rolling down my face. They brought him over to me and without a word, they placed him on my lap and I scooped him up. I held him against my chest, my head bowed to take in his smells, the soft fluff of his hair against my cheek, and I sobbed loud, chest-heaving sobs. I didn't care who else was in that room. At that moment I knew why I was still alive. And nothing else mattered. The rest of the room fell silent and then cleared out.

Colston visited for a week. It felt so good to have him there and I do think it helped me become a little more functional. They gave me an electric wheelchair. I would put Colston on my lap and we would whiz around the hallways in that chair. He just loved it. He would giggle hysterically as we made lap after lap around that linoleum-lined track. This was also terrifying because while we zoomed around the hospital I was controlling the gauge and also trying to hold on to my son with one arm. I would use my leg stump to hold him up in my lap to keep him from falling forward and prevent myself from running over him in the wheelchair.

Something changed for me during Colston's visit. I felt I could do more and I had a fundamental shift in my mental outlook. I wasn't a pathetic patient anymore. I was a father. I had a purpose again. There was so much meaning in something as simple as using what had been my leg to keep him from falling out of my lap. My physical therapist, Bob, could see how positively Colston affected my treatment.

"If I said to you I want you to ride around in this wheelchair with a fifteen-pound bag of rice in your lap, and if I told you to use what is left of your leg to hold on to that bag and keep it from rolling forward, you would have told me, 'No way. I'm not doing that.' You would have said that was excruciatingly painful. But with Colston in place of the bag of rice, your pain disappears," Bob said.

He was right. I held tightly to Colston and we roamed all over the hospital. If he wanted to go somewhere, we went.

My parents had a room at the Mologne House, a place where the families of wounded soldiers can stay while their soldier heals. It's within the grounds of Walter Reed, so family members can walk to visit their loved one. While Colston was in town he and my sisters stayed there with my parents. This was enough of an incentive to get me outside the confines of the hospital for the first time. I wanted to be with Colston as much as I could. I never wanted to let him go.

My parents helped me wheel over to their room one night and picked me up to help me onto one of the beds. I was in a lot of pain but I was there with my boy. I wasn't going to let the pain get in the way of that. We snuggled on the bed and watched cartoons. I could still scoop him up in my arm and feed him his bottle before bed. It was the best thing to happen in a long time. Then it was getting late and I said, "I want to stay here in this room. I want to stay here with Colston."

My mom went to ask one of the nurses and she said, "Yes, that is a huge progress. If there is room for him with you all, let him stay in the room. If you need anything, let us know."

This was huge. I was still at Walter Reed. There was still medical staff nearby should I need it, but this was a mental victory. I was out of that tiny room. I was taking one step back into the real world. I was back with my child and reminded that I had a reason to fight and heal.

Of course, with my parents, my three sisters, and Colston already sharing that one room, adding me to the mix made it just too crowded. So my sister Sara volunteered to sleep in my hospital room. When we were ready to settle in for the night, she headed back over to the hospital and climbed into my hospital bed. She tucked the pillows all around herself, got comfortable, pulled up the blankets, and fell asleep. She wasn't asleep long, however. She was in a hospital, after all. Throughout the night, in a hospital, doctors and nurses go on rounds. In the middle of the night a group of doctors and nurses on the night shift all shuffled into the room, talking about my case, and startled Sara from her slumber. She poked her head out of the covers. The doctors all collectively gasped and one of them said, "Who are you?"

She nervously laughed and said, "Oh! Sorry. I'm Noah's sister Sara. Noah stayed at the Mologne House tonight with our family."

"Oh, he did?" the doctor replied, sounding very surprised but pleased. "Well, that's huge!"

They were still standing in the room so Sara said, "Yeah, it is. So I am sleeping in here." She waited for them to get the hint. They started laughing and told her they would let her get back to sleep.

As time passed, I learned more and more about the culture that comes with being an injured veteran. There are a lot of really wonderful people and organizations to help veterans returning from war. Right about the time I started to really move forward in my recovery, two women came by and introduced themselves. They explained that they raise money to help injured veterans with various needs. They asked if there was anything I or my family needed. I said, "No thank you, I'm all good." But my sisters piped up and said, "He needs clothes. He doesn't have anything." The women smiled and said they'd be back. They came back with some sweatpants and a shirt and then announced that they were taking us to the mall. This would be my first time leaving the campus of Walter Reed, my first real trip out of the hospital. We were all excited. Leaving the hospital was a big step for me but my poor sisters had been cooped up much of the time with me in there as well. I was a little nervous, but I owed it to them to push aside my anxiety.

We decided that the electric wheelchair would be too heavy and too much trouble to get in and out of the car, so Jennifer wheeled me down to the front door where the ladies were waiting in their car. With very little assistance, Jennifer was able to get me from that chair into the car and we were off to the mall. When we arrived, my sisters pulled the wheelchair out of the trunk and placed it next to the car door. They opened the door and Jennifer leaned down and with one swift motion lifted me up like a nearly weightless child and placed me in the chair. I laughed it off.

"My sister's strong. She's really strong," I boasted on her behalf.

Sara, Katherine, and Jennifer were laughing the whole time because I didn't realize how scrawny I was, how much weight I had lost. Jennifer could pick me up with no problem because I practically weighed nothing at all. But through the laughter, I felt a pang of guilt. I am the brother of three sisters. It was my job to protect and care for them. Yet here I was, barely able to take care of myself.

*   *   *

I was born a superhero. By age four I was convinced of that fact. I was Alabama's very own Superman. I even had a uniform. I was legit. Every morning when I hopped out of bed, I would pull on my brown leather cowboy boots and march out of my room and down the hall in nothing but shorts and those boots. No need for a shirt. As I stood stoically with my hands on my hips, my mom would adorn me with my cape. Okay, in reality she wrapped a baby blue bath towel around my shoulders that she probably grabbed out of the laundry basket and fastened the ends of which together under my chin with a diaper pin. And all right, I didn't have abs of steel. I was a chubby kid. But never mind that, I was fierce, independent, and superhuman, a pint-sized caped crusader complete with cowboy boots because, well, I was in Alabama, after all. This superhero was a little bit country. Like any good superhero I even had my own sidekick—Hoss the German shepherd. Everywhere I went, Hoss followed. And even as a toddler I went wherever I wanted to go, whenever I wanted. Hoss and I were always on the hunt for our next adventure. Hoss and I took off as we pleased when I was as young as three years old. This stressed out my parents and older sister Jennifer quite often, but I had a curiosity that couldn't be contained.

I couldn't fly like Superman but I fixed that problem, too. I had my very own superpowered vehicle. I drove a ride-on toy postal truck. In essence, it was my first jeep. Be it on foot or in my mail truck, Hoss and I were always out on patrol for our next adventure or any danger that might come our way.

One day the Galloways got a little more excitement than we were prepared for. We moved around a lot and at this point we were living in a trailer park in Auburn, Alabama. Hoss and I were out in the front yard on our regular patrol while my older sister Jennifer and younger sister Sara were playing by themselves. Sara was three years old and I guess she decided she wanted to go for a ride. My dad's blue truck was out in front of the house and apparently he'd forgotten about the parking brake. The truck was in gear as Sara managed to pull the door open and muscle herself up into the cab. As she climbed in and got situated she kicked the truck out of gear with her tiny sneakered foot. The truck started rolling down the driveway toward a ditch. Jennifer started screaming.

Faster than a speeding bullet I leapt into action! I ran toward her, blue cape flying in the wind behind me. I reached the truck. I grabbed on to the door frame of the open passenger side of the truck. I told Sara everything would be okay, and I stuck my heels down into the mud and pulled back with all my might. The mud was spewing from either side of my firmly planted boots as I started to slide along with the truck. I never lost my grip and I am convinced I was able to slow the roll down enough for Mom and Dad to come running out of the house. Dad jumped up into the truck and was able to throw the brake to stop the truck while Mom scooped up Sara. Super Noah saved the day. At least I wanted to believe that.

*　*　*

With my sisters at the helm of my chair, we maneuvered through the mall just fine. We were having fun as a family—probably for the first time since before I deployed. At one store I picked out some pants and heard my sisters snickering in the corner behind me. They turned around triumphantly brandishing a T-shirt they'd found that had a silhouette of a bride and groom with a jagged line down the middle. In the kind of type font you'd find in a video game were the words "Game Over." I was in the middle of my divorce and they thought this was funny. I did not. I wasn't there yet, but I didn't let it upset me. My sisters are goofy and subscribe to the theory that humor is the best way to deal with tough things.

We went into a shoe store and I wheeled myself over to a pair of sneakers. I picked up one of the shoes and looked at it more closely. It was a New Balance sneaker. One of the women from the charity leaned over and looked, too.

"Do you like these shoes?" she asked.

"Yeah, I do. These shoes look good but you know, they're like ninety dollars," I said with a shrug. That was too much money for a pair of sneakers and I knew it.

"The ones over here are about forty dollars. They look pretty similar," I said, pointing to another pair placed next to the New Balances I'd been admiring.

"Well, yes, but do you like these?" she asked, holding up the original pair and smiling.

"Yeah, they look great, but these shoes are probably better," I said pointing to the cheaper pair.

At this point my sisters noticed the conversation. Sara walked over to us and said, "Noah, get the pair you want."

"Yeah, but these are so much cheaper," I said, again trying to emphasize that the second pair was the more practical decision.

"Noah, get the pair you want," Sara almost yelled. She gestured at the shoes in a fashion that indicated I should absolutely get the New Balance pair. She took the hint from Sara and didn't ask again. Instead she just asked what size I wore. As soon as the salesman found the right size, the very generous woman marched toward the cashier with the more expensive pair of sneakers in their hands.

I continued to make little improvements each day. I think this was a big relief for my family. We'd never been a family to talk openly about our emotions and my injury proved to be the ultimate test for us. I mean my injury was real and was in everyone's faces. But I'm sure that as I began to improve, they were feeling better each day, too. No one was used to me needing help. Each step I made toward independence made my family breathe a little easier.

One day Mom came to my hospital room and sat down on the edge of the bed, facing me. I could already see tears forming in the corners of her eye. She said she had something to tell me. Whatever she was about to say was hard for her to get out. Her voice was noticeably shaky and her chin quivered as she spoke.

"Noah, I've got to leave and get back to work. And besides, I am helping you too much. You need to be doing more on your own." She couldn't hold it back at all and by the time she finished the second sentence the tears were streaming down her rosy cheeks.

After a few deep breaths, she continued, "But your dad is here, and you know Dad, he's not that helpful." We both laughed at that as she leaned forward on the bed and grabbed my hand. I told her that I understood and that yes, it was probably best because Dad would help but not too much.

After Mom left, I was doing well enough that I transitioned from the hospital room to sharing the room at the Mologne House with my dad. He was the only one of the family left on a permanent basis. It was just Dad and me in that one room. At times, that was pretty miserable! I would wake up in the morning and he'd be sitting there at this little table in the hotel room, drinking his coffee and just looking at me. I get it now; he was just being a dad. But while it was happening, I thought, *What are you looking at, Dad? Quit staring at me.* And then he also washed my clothes, which astounded me. He was doing things I'd never seen the man do before. So even with his annoying staring at me while I slept thing, I was grateful he was there.

In addition to my obviously missing limbs, my right leg was also pretty damaged from the explosion. The doctors removed a huge chunk of muscle out of my inner thigh where a piece of metal had entered and exited my body. That surgery left a small scar on the outside of my thigh but it was healing. My calf muscle, however, had a hole in it that was taking forever to heal. That wound had to be kept bandaged up and required a continuous process of cleaning and rebandaging. As the nurses carefully removed the bandages for cleaning, the amount of pus and gore that would ooze out was gross. The hole was very deep. But eventually my leg started to heal and I was able to regain some movement in it. They would try to have me stand, but my leg was too weak. I couldn't pick up the front of my foot. My big toe would droop. But we kept at it and little by little I improved.

Eventually I gained enough strength to use the regular wheelchair. We removed the footpads, so I could just use the strength I had to scoot my leg along with the chair as I used my right arm to turn the wheel. I found I liked that even better than the electric chair, because being able to use it was a tangible measure of improvement. It was also easier to move around in that smaller and lighter chair. I got better and better at it and more and more self-sufficient. I even was able to get myself to and from the hospital for doctor visits and treatments.

It wasn't long before I was being fitted for my prosthetic leg. A prosthetic leg has several parts. There is a knee unit and a foot, but the most important part is the socket. The socket needs to fit perfectly over the residual limb. The pressure can't all be at the bottom. If it fits snugly it removes the pressure from the end of the stump.

First, they made what's called a test socket. The test socket is made from a type of plastic that can be heated and molded. I put it on and I could tell them where I felt pressure and they could adjust it. The test socket also helps determine if it's the correct size or if that, too, needs to be adjusted. Even though it was molded specifically for me, it's not a one-and-done kind of process. They have to do a little work to make it a perfect fit. After all the kinks have been worked out and the test socket is molded just right, they can take that mold and make the final prosthetic leg out of carbon fiber.

I was excited to get this process started. I had mastered the wheelchair and I was wheeling myself all over the place. Pushing myself in the chair also made my body stronger. I remember one day I rolled down from the Mologne House to go to one of my appointments in the hospital. I caught up to a marine who still had both his arms but was missing both legs. We rolled along, side by side, and were just chatting. His mom was walking behind us. We got inside the door of one of the hospital buildings and for some reason I thought I needed to go left and he went right. I told him I'd see him later and he turned right and went on his way. I started to head to the left and realized wait, no, that's not correct. The elevator was to the right. I turned around and headed back in the other direction. The marine and his mom were in front of me now and I heard him ask, "Mom, will you push me?" She answered "You can do it."

"Yes, but it makes my hands hurt and I sweat when I wear my gloves," he replied. His mother shrugged her shoulders and resumed her position behind his chair to push him the rest of the way. I had to stifle my laughter. Clearly this guy didn't want his mom to push him in front of me. I only had one arm and I was managing just fine. But when I wasn't around, his hands hurt too much. It made me realize just how far I'd come.

I was headed into the final fitting of my leg. I'd gone through the test socket phase and my leg was finally ready. I was so excited! I walked into the physical therapy lab and shouted, "Man, I cannot wait to put this leg on and walk!"

My physical therapist, Bob, and the prosthetist exchanged nervous glances. My right leg was still pretty weak and by all normal standards, I should not be able to walk right away. But then, of course, I never like to be like everyone else. They had me wheel over to the parallel bars to attach my new leg.

"We're just going to have you stand for now," said Bob.

"Nah, I'm walking." I offered up my best shit-eating grin.

"Let's just see how it feels," Bob replied with some firmness.

I stood up and said, "I feel good. I feel really good."

Bob relented and they let me try to walk. They put a belt around me so that Bob could hold on to me as I walked the parallel bars. Most guys can use the parallel bars for support. I only have one arm so that only helped me so much. Good thing I didn't really need them. I started walking without faltering right away.

"Yeah, this feels good. I feel good. You can back up," I told them.

They backed up and I started walking by myself, holding on with one hand. Then, feeling bolder, I lifted my hand off the bar. I took a step. And then another step. I was walking without any help. I walked up and down those parallel bars the very first day I put on my leg.

I did all this with an audience. Dad and Uncle Johnny were right there with me, watching and cheering me on. They were so excited. Uncle Johnny snapped a picture and sent it to my mom back home in Alabama. And as any proud mom would do, she sent that picture to everyone she knew. That picture went the pre-viral version of viral! It was a triumphant snapshot. I was walking again. And not only that, I was wearing those shiny new New Balance shoes the nice ladies had given me. As the picture made the rounds through my mom's friends and friends of her friends and friends of friends of friends, somehow it ended up with people at New Balance. They reached out to my mom to ask what sizes of shoe Colston and I wore. She told them and then soon after that, Colston and I had matching sneakers.

I made several laps up and down those bars and then I told them, "All right, I want to wear this leg out of here today."

They told me, not so fast. I protested but then they explained that a little more work would be required before I could take it home. Most people walk on crutches at first and then move down to a cane. With only one arm, crutches wouldn't do me a whole lot of good. So I reluctantly agreed to come back a few more times until I was steady with a cane on my own. After I gained some independence with the wheelchair and I could control where I went, I had stopped going to physical therapy. I hadn't seen the point. But now that they were dangling that leg in front of me—that freedom—you'd better believe I went for it.

I went to physical therapy every day to walk on that leg. After about a week, I convinced them to let me take it home. Once Bob and his crew caved on that, I never went to physical therapy again. I was done. I was too busy walking. I worked on my walking every minute of the day and everywhere I could walk. I noticed a lot of other patients would wear their leg in physical therapy and then take it off after and go back to the wheelchair. Not me. Once I was up and moving, I did not want to be in that chair anymore unless I'd worn myself out. Every step I took was an improvement. Every step counted.

Whenever people came to visit me at Walter Reed, everyone wanted to see the same things in D.C. Everyone wanted to go to the monuments, so I would go. It was a struggle but I was out there doing it. My friend Terry, his wife, Tracie, and their two boys, Brandon and Ryan, drove up from Alabama to see me and we went to see the monuments. I walked the whole day with the cane and when we got into a parking deck heading to the car suddenly I handed the twelve-year-old my cane and said, "Here, Brandon! Hold this."

Terry looked back at me over his shoulder. "What are you about to do?"

I said, "I think I can walk without it." I took a few steps and realized I was steady without the cane. "Yeah, I'm good. I don't need that cane. I feel great."

I was doing the work on my own. I wasn't going to physical therapy, but occasionally I'd pass my physical therapist in the hallway. He knew he couldn't get me to come back but he still felt the need to help me. So he'd correct me in the hall.

"You know you're walking too stiffly in your upper body. Your shirt should wrinkle. Your right hand should be reaching out to your left leg going out and your left arm should be reached out to your right foot going out. Your shirt should be wrinkling," he said.

"All right. Gotcha." So I start swinging both arms, even the one that's not there. I'm swinging and I'm walking. And then I got to where I would get behind people in the hallway and mimic the way they walked. Now I had to be careful. I had to double-check to make sure the person I was mimicking wasn't another amputee, because we were all over the place there. I was constantly busting my ass to improve my walking. And that's what I did.

CHAPTER 5

A Blast from the Past

WHILE I WAS still bedridden and my mouth was wired shut, the hospital gave me a laptop to use. It was old and not fancy, but I could get on the Internet and I could email people. This was a big help at that point, as I was still really fragile. Brandi had just left and I was still pretty incapacitated. I felt very alone. My family was there with me, but I was still feeling raw and cut off emotionally from the world I knew. I would sit in the dark in my room and *tap, tap, tap* out emails to friends, as best I could, with one hand.

I didn't know it but word traveled fast that I was injured. I was hearing from people I hadn't talked to in ages. One of my childhood friends, Seth, reached out as soon as he knew. He was also making sure other kids we grew up with heard, too. Seth is one of those old friends you know you can count on even if a lot of time passes between visits. So reconnecting with him was really good for me. I know now just how fortunate I was that it happened early on in my recovery.

Seth suggested I get on MySpace. He said he'd create an account for me. I thought it was pretty lame, but I wasn't really up for much of a protest at the time. Through this early social media platform, the people we grew up with were reaching out and reconnecting. I was typing with one hand and I couldn't open my mouth, yet I had a whole new way to communicate and feel connected to people. One of these childhood friends was Tracy Ennis. I noticed right away that she still had her maiden name. We had dated in middle school, but I hadn't seen her in ten years. I wondered what she looked like now. I clicked on her page and looked through her pictures. I thought, *Aw, she looks adorable. Just like she always did.*

Quickly we went from MySpace to exchanging emails. We started emailing a lot. She was very sweet. She was so concerned about me and told me over and over how sorry she was to hear about my injury. I was reconnecting with a lot of old friends, but she was different. There was a deeper connection almost immediately.

A little while later, Seth and Tracy decided they wanted to come visit me. Tracy spent just about all the money she had on her plane ticket and splitting a hotel room with Seth, but she was determined to come. And I was excited to have something to look forward to.

About two weeks before their visit I went through some big changes. The wires binding my mouth shut were finally removed. That procedure was a pretty big ordeal. The doctors had sewn the wires between the gum line and my teeth, top and bottom, in a zigzag pattern. They had an assistant who was learning the process come in to learn on my mouth how to remove them.

Thankfully, because of this I was given a little extra medication beforehand, because she took some pliers and just yanked. I felt the wire whip around every one of my teeth and through my gums. My gums had grown over the wires in some spots, so this was pretty painful!

Two days before Seth and Tracy arrived I had an appointment with the ear, nose, and throat doctor who had treated my jaw. Since my jaw had been forced shut for a pretty long time, I struggled to use it again. The doctors were concerned because it now wasn't opening very wide.

"Have you been doing your jaw exercises?" the doctor asked.

"What are you talking about?" I asked.

"Working on making your jaw open up more?" he said.

"Y'all didn't tell me to do that!" I replied. Clearly I needed to work on that. I didn't even realize that my mouth was barely opening, because I had gotten used to it being shut for so long. And because I'd had my mouth sewn shut all this time I was living off IV nutrients and Ensure through a feeding tube and was really scrawny.

Seth and Tracy arrived on St. Patrick's Day weekend. They got a room at the cheapest hotel they could find nearby and we did our best to keep things low budget. We had plans to go out to dinner later on that first night, but for lunch we thought we'd just do something cheap. Dad told us there was a McDonald's across the street, so they helped me into the car and we used the drive-through window. This was to be the first solid food I put into my body since Iraq. It had been three months. I told them to just order me a cheeseburger. We hadn't even pulled out of the drive-through when I'd opened my mouth as wide as I could, which was maybe an inch or two, and nibbled away at that cheeseburger like a rabid squirrel.

"This is amazing!" I shouted as I crammed the rest of that burger in my mouth and crumbled up the yellow paper wrapper.

"Go back through the drive-through!" I demanded.

Seth and Tracy turned to look at me.

"Go back through the drive-through," I said again, this time motioning with my hand toward the line.

I ate four more cheeseburgers right there on the spot. Sure, in hindsight, maybe it was not the best way to reintroduce the body to solid food, but I loved it. McDonald's then became my obsession. I'd never really eaten McDonald's before I got injured and I don't really eat it now, but it was the first thing I ate after they opened my jaws up, and I couldn't get enough of it. I went every afternoon. Forget physical therapy. I was exercising my jaw on quarter-pounders.

Later that night as we were hanging out in my room at the Mologne House, Seth, out of the blue, started talking about how tough he thought I was. He was impressed with how I was able to live through my injury and that I was recovering so well. It wasn't a particularly emotional speech, but something in Seth's simple but kind words set me off.

"But I've lost everything: my career, two limbs, my marriage. Life sucks," I blurted out. Tracy and Seth stared at me, stunned. I muttered a few more words before the tears started. It wasn't just a few wayward tears. I was sobbing. Seth and Tracy started crying as well. It was such a shock. It wasn't like I felt those emotions building up or boiling over. I had done such a good job of pushing them down and hiding them from everyone else, I had fooled myself, too. Tracy walked over and sat down next to me. Without a word she wrapped her arms around me and pulled me into a tight hug. She was rocking me back and forth gently as we both cried. That was the first moment where I recognized exactly how scared I was of my new life. But at the same time I felt so much comfort. I was in a safe place with two friends I'd known since childhood. I let my guard down, and for Tracy and me, that was the precise moment our bond formed. These two old friends provided me with the outlet I didn't know that I needed so badly.

All three of us had a good cry just before my dad came back to the room. Leave it to Dad to change the subject.

"Noah, you need to take a shower. It's been about a week. You need to be bathing, son," he said without at all noticing that the timing might not have been the best.

I had gone through a lot of surgeries. I had a lot of scars. Just having water touch my skin hurt badly. So, no, I wasn't showering very often. But come on, did he have to say that right in front of Seth and, more important, Tracy? I was trying so hard to impress her. I tried to nip the conversation in the bud as quickly as possible. "Gotcha, Dad! Okay!" I said. I looked at Dad with an expression that suggested he drop it. Thankfully Tracy didn't seem to flinch.

The second night of their trip, after a day of running around with them, I went back to their hotel. We were walking down the hallway and I said, "I bet I could run." I was clearly trying to show off for Tracy. So I started jumping and swinging the leg out down the hallway as fast as I could.

"You gotta stop! I don't want you getting hurt!" Seth yelled.

I was making him very nervous. "Okay, okay," I said and gestured that I would stop. But I didn't. I tried again.

"What are you doing?" Seth shouted. I looked over at Tracy and she was laughing. Mission accomplished.

I finally stopped and Seth was able to breathe again. We went back to the room and settled in for the night. The room had two beds. Seth was in one and Tracy and I climbed into the other one. The three of us sat up and laughed and talked for a while.

After Seth fell asleep and started snoring, Tracy and I finally had some time alone. We talked a bit and then I mustered up my nerve and leaned in to kiss her for the first time in ten years. It felt so good. So right. Just one kiss and then we talked a little while more. Finally I said, rather sheepishly, "I'd like to keep talking to you."

She smiled and replied, "I'd like that, too." We curled up together and fell asleep. I am certain I slept with a smile on my face all night long.

The next day I took Seth and Tracy to see the monuments. I was a little sore and tired from all of the activity—and probably from the running the night before. Seth and Tracy suggested we take the wheelchair along. I bristled and stubbornly protested.

"Just take the wheelchair," Seth pleaded with me. Tracy said, "We would be honored to push you in the wheelchair. Let's just take it so you're not overstressed walking on the leg."

My stump was hurting, so I finally gave in and agreed. As I grumbled about it a bit more, Seth folded the wheelchair up and loaded it into my dad's car. I recognized that walking the National Mall without the chair wasn't really doable yet. They were right.

Tracy pushed me along as we walked the paths, which were studded with cherry trees in full bloom. It was gorgeous. Seth buzzed around us, back and forth, running his mouth. Seth is a talker, like I am. That's what's funny about our friendship. Seth loves to talk about Seth and Noah likes to talk about Noah. We get along great.

Seth wasn't paying much attention to us. He wandered off to go look at something and suddenly I felt agitated. I was replaying the previous night's kiss over and over in my head and it bothered me.

"I don't need your sympathy," I spat out rudely to Tracy.

"What are you talking about?" she asked.

"Last night when we kissed. I don't want your sympathy. In fact, when y'all leave, we don't have to keep talking." I didn't look her in the eye when I said it.

"What are you talking about?" she asked again, this time a little taken aback.

"You kissed me last night because you feel sorry for me. Because I've been injured. I lost two of my limbs, I'm going through a divorce, that's why you did it. And I don't need that. I don't want that."

She was visibly upset at this point. "If you think I kissed you out of sympathy, one, you're an asshole; two, you're just being a jerk; and three, you're mean. And that's very insensitive to me as a person." She crossed her arms and turned away from me.

"Well, why did you do it?" I asked.

She turned and looked me straight in the eyes. "Because I like you. I don't care that you're missing two limbs."

The conversation went on for a while like that, with me being a jerk. When Seth came back we stopped talking, but you could cut the tension with a knife at that point. The next chance we had where Seth walked off, I told Tracy to stop pushing the chair. I turned it around and told her I was sorry.

"I don't know how to react. I really like you and I thought you were just doing that out of sympathy, and I'm sorry I said those things. If you really want to keep talking, I would like that," I said. My voice was much softer. I was ashamed I'd lashed out at her.

She said, "I do," and leaned down and gave me a kiss.

CHAPTER 6

Transition to Independence

(May–August 2006)

AFTER TRACY and Seth's visit I felt ready to be on my own. I told Dad he could go on home.

He was a little shocked when I suggested it, but he finally agreed. We decided to rent a trailer and hook it up to my dad's truck to take home a bunch of my things. Over the months of my stay, people had sent care packages or get-well gifts and it all had to get back to Alabama somehow. So this was a good time to do it.

Before he left, my dad was still harping about the amount of medication I was taking. Pain medication in particular. "Noah, you have two options in this situation. You're either gonna be a legalized drug addict or you're gonna quit taking all this pain medication and get on with your life." Now, my dad is not a doctor, as I've said, and he should not have been doling out this kind of advice. In fact, in hindsight it was very dangerous. But at the time, what he said hit me hard and I decided to quit my pain medications cold turkey. I was on about a dozen pills a day, so when he said that, I said, "Okay, I am going to quit today." And I did quit, ill-advisedly, that very day.

I remember that by the third night of no sleep I was suffering from withdrawal. I was awake and Dad was in the other bed snoring loudly. I'd sat at the end of the bed and just stared into oblivion. Every time I turned my head I saw tracers. I was shivering. I was whimpering like a baby. It was as if I was having nightmares while I was wide awake. I'd look over at Dad just snoring and sleeping without a care in the world. His snores bounced off the walls and echoed in the room. I dug my nails into the mattress and clenched my jaw as the anger bubbled up inside me. How could he sleep through all of this? After two terrifying nights like that, I gave up on trying to sleep. It was better to just stay awake. Four days went by with no sleep. Early in the morning on the fifth day I finally felt a release from the shivering and the crying and was able to doze off. But as soon as my eyes finally shut, I heard my dad calling my name.

"Noah, you have an appointment you gotta make," he said as he shook my shoulder.

"Gawd dang. I don't want to go," I said. I was just so drained. But I pulled myself out of bed and trudged to the hospital for my appointment.

The doctor sat opposite me and looked at his notes as he talked. I was concentrating really hard on keeping my eyes open.

After what seemed like a million years he looked up and said, "All right, I am going to give you some new prescriptions for your medications."

"Oh, I quit all that," I said nonchalantly.

"You did what?" the doctor yelled and almost dropped his clipboard on the floor.

"Yeah, I quit."

"You quit? When?" he asked, clearly alarmed.

"Four days ago," I said flatly.

"NO! NO! NO! NO!" he shouted. And then he was a blur, flying all around me checking my blood pressure and other vitals. He looked terrified.

"You can't just do that. You're on a serious dosage of some potentially dangerous stuff. You can't just quit. How do you feel? How are things going?"

"I'm good, I'm good. I haven't slept in a few days but I'm pretty tired. I'm pretty sure I'm gonna sleep as soon as this appointment is over," I said while I shrugged off more poking and prodding.

He pulled out his pen and prescription pad again and said, "I'm going to put you back on your medications and wean you off properly."

"No! The last few days I've had were miserable and I'm not going back. I'm off it. I'm done. I'm not taking it."

He wasn't happy but I wasn't changing my mind. He could write the prescriptions all he wanted. I wasn't going to take them. And I told him that. I left, went to my room, and passed out. I slept, finally, and after that I was fine.

After I got off the pain medication I knew for sure now that I would be all right. Dad and I were going to drive home together, so I had to follow protocol and get permission to leave. I was still considered active duty, so I couldn't just come and go as I pleased. I was granted leave and we packed up the truck and trailer and got on the road. This would be my first trip since my injury and my first time at home. I was both excited and anxious.

Dad and I had to go through Clarksville, Tennessee, on our way to Alabama. When the divorce was finalized, Brandi moved home to her parents' house but I still owned our home there. It had been sitting empty all this time. I needed to check on the house and pack up some things I needed. After the pit stop in Clarksville, it was straight on to Birmingham.

For the most part, I felt fine. But I had developed a case of paranoia after my injury. It was a form of PTSD that made me jumpy and on edge. I hid it pretty well but every now and then, I lost it. Dad was at the wheel and I dozed in the passenger seat as we cut through Nashville. Traffic was just bumper-to-bumper. Stop and go, stop and go. All of a sudden someone cut in front of us, and Dad slammed on the brakes. My right leg bumped against the dashboard. It completely freaked me out. I was thinking, *The last thing I want to do is get in a wreck and lose another limb.* I completely lost it and blew up at my father.

"Why did you do that? I can't get injured again! Pull over. I'll drive!" I screamed.

Dad is not the kind of person who would have ever taken that kind of behavior from me in the past, but I think he understood the paranoia. I'd asked him while I was in the hospital, "Did you ever think one of your kids would ever lose a limb?"

And he said, "No, it never crossed my mind. I was always more afraid I would lose another limb."

It wasn't until later that I realized how great it was of him that he kept his cool and understood where I was coming from. He just let me freak out and let me drive. I think in some ways it was the same kind of lesson he taught me as a child without ever saying a word. I watched him just get on with things with one arm. He never made a fuss about it. It was an example that growing up I didn't know I'd need eventually.

So I got in the driver's seat and we continued on our way. After a while we stopped at a gas station to stretch our legs and get some snacks. I grabbed a lemon-lime Gatorade and Dad grabbed something to drink and we got back in the car. I turned the car on, so the air and the radio were going as I tried and tried to get my Gatorade bottle open, but the top was too big and I couldn't quite get my fingers to grab it, hold it, and twist it open. My finger strength just wasn't there yet. So I put it between my legs and tried to hold it still while I twisted the top. I heard the creak of release as I managed to break the seal of the plastic orange cap but my legs were squeezing the bottle so hard that the bright yellow liquid squirted all over me. "Crap!" I yelled. I heard my dad snicker. I turned to look at him and he smirked while holding a can of Coke in his hand.

"And that's why I drink out of a can," he declared with a smug grin. *Click. Fizzzz.* With one hand, Dad popped that can open and took a big slug of his soda.

The trip home was good for me. I was happy to be home and to see Colston and my family. I was also very happy to see Tracy. At this point we were talking on the phone every night. And I was really ready to be at home. I'd spent all of those days and nights on the other end of the line from her just imagining the life I could have once I was out of the hospital for good. She'd helped me to transition from feeling I'd lost everything to realizing that I had something and someone to come home to. Of course, there was my son, but with every phone call Tracy and I got closer and adapting to my new normal seemed less overwhelming.

But being home for the first time also was a little strange. It was 2006, and images of injured veterans weren't the norm yet. I was at Walter Reed when it was the busiest, and so I was a part of the first wave of injured veterans from this war, the first injured veterans that my generation had experienced. It can be hard not to stare at a guy missing an arm and a leg. When I was at Walter Reed that wasn't an issue. Everyone was missing limbs. But out here, in the real world, things were different. Nobody was rude, but they looked. They watched. Everywhere I went people were in shock, because suddenly the war was real for them. I tried to justify the staring, knowing that if somebody walked past me missing two limbs I'd look, too. But it does make you self-conscious and anxious to feel like everyone's watching your every move. I found that I developed a habit of constantly thinking when I was walking, *Don't fall. Don't fall. Don't fall.* It was all I thought about. I was so insecure about myself that it was really hard to go places.

After that visit home, the remainder of my time at Walter Reed and in the Army became a waiting game, and I was done playing by anybody else's rules but my own. I no longer asked permission to leave or followed procedure. Because I was still in the Army and a part of the medical hold platoon, I was required to show up for formation every morning, Monday through Friday.

Formation in medical hold carried a different, grimmer purpose than it did when on post back at Fort Campbell, Kentucky. Here it was how they kept track of everyone. They made sure everybody was there and nobody had disappeared, committed suicide, or died overnight. We'd all gather on a basketball court on the grounds of Walter Reed. There were plenty of injured guys in wheelchairs, but as I'd come to find out, a lot of medical hold included guys avoiding duty. I had no respect for that. Not every job in the military requires you to enter a war zone, but if you are in one of those jobs and you sidestep combat and avoid deployment, I feel you do not deserve to wear the uniform. This was the first time I realized that people were doing that and I wanted nothing to do with these men. It changed me in a way. I felt like I no longer belonged in the Army at all. I couldn't work under and with men I didn't respect. I no longer felt an obligation to play by the rules.

So each day I walked into formation and I sat in the back. I didn't even bother standing up. After formation everyone went off to various appointments. I lied and came up with a list of appointments every day and instead I went straight back to my room. I slept most of the time. On Fridays I said the same thing but I went straight to my car, where I already had a packed bag, and I would head out on that ten-hour drive home to Birmingham. I did that every weekend. I would spend time with Colston and with Tracy and then I'd drive back all night on Sundays to be in formation Monday morning.

I felt those trips were an extension of my own brand of physical therapy. I was pushing myself every week. It would hurt my leg to sit that long with the prosthetic on, so sometimes I would ease it off in the car. Other times I would just pull over and stand up on it for a while. If it got to where sitting in it hurt, I would move around. These trips also helped me ease back into civilian life. Each week I got a little bit more of a taste of being out in the real world again.

During this time, I formed a peculiar addiction to Cracker Barrel. I am proud to say that I have eaten at every Cracker Barrel between Washington, D.C., and Birmingham, probably more than once. I would sit by myself, and while I was eating I would look at everyone else eating, and I would pick a table to concentrate on. One time it was a mom and three daughters and they were just laughing and joking around. The girls were between the ages of six and twelve, and they all were having such a good time. When I got my check I said, "Get me that one, too." I paid for my meal and theirs and after that I would sometimes pay for others.

I did have one not-so-positive experience at my beloved Cracker Barrel on one of those many visits. I stopped in as I usually did and I wanted a steak. When the hostess brought me to my table, I situated myself as I always did. I sat where people were on my right side. I found there were fewer stares that way. Sitting this way, no one could tell I was missing my left arm and left leg. Only my right arm and right leg were visible. The waitress came to take my order and I said, "I want the steak. Can you get it cut up for me?"

She paused for a moment and stared at me. Just a second but long enough that I noticed before she replied, "Uh, cut up. Yeah. Okay." As she walked away I heard her mumble, "Can't cut his own steak." Now, in her defense, she didn't see that I was missing an arm and a leg.

A little while went by and she brought out the steak. It was whole. I looked up at her and said, "The steak's not cut."

"Yeah, the cook said they couldn't do it and I was gonna do it but they said I wasn't allowed to so you're gonna have to cut your own steak," she replied.

"Really? Okay." I stabbed the steak with my fork, picked it up, and started gnawing at it. I ate my food and my waitress never returned to check on me or refill my water. There was no more attention paid to my table whatsoever. When she finally came back with the check I said, "I'd like to see your manager." The manager came over to my table and I stood up, all of my body now fully visible and my disability exposed.

"I asked your waitress to cut up my steak and she had a problem with cutting it up for me. She said the cook said they wouldn't do it and she wasn't allowed to do it. I find that hard to believe." The manager looked shocked and embarrassed and I watched him look down to where my left hand should be for a few seconds.

I continued, "I don't want a free meal, I'm paying for my meal. But I want to tell you if I had come in here with two arms and I said I want my steak cut, that's how it should be prepared. That's good service."

"I agree," he managed to say.

"Well, all right, maybe you can work on your staff." With that I walked off. I went to the counter and paid for my meal and walked out. I got back in the car and called my mom. The story sure did make her mad, but she's my mom and that's how I'd expect she'd react. I didn't think anything more of it and I continued my drive home. A little while later Mom called back.

"Which Cracker Barrel was it, Noah?" she asked.

"I don't know, Mom," I answered.

"Well, I have Cracker Barrel headquarters on the other line and they want to know which one it is," said Mom.

"Mom, I really don't know where I was. I've eaten at so many of them."

She said okay and hung up. She called back a little while later.

"They are sending you four Golden Tickets that will pay for four meals," she said triumphantly.

I started laughing and told her thank you. And what do you know, I got those four Golden Tickets in the mail as promised. Tracy's brother was a teenager at the time so one evening I told him to grab two friends to go eat. I took them out and told them to get whatever they wanted, including desserts.

I want to be clear that I still eat at Cracker Barrel on a regular basis. The lesson here is one bad apple doesn't spoil the barrel, pun intended.

I don't think I fully realized before that incident just how visible my injuries were. Once people notice my injuries they are able to grasp that certain things will be harder for me to do. But there were so many other veterans coming back home with conditions not visible to the naked eye. They were going to need help, too.

CHAPTER 7

I'm Out of the Army Now

I DIDN'T FOLLOW PROTOCOL. I wasn't going to physical therapy. I was leaving every weekend. I couldn't stand the unit I was assigned to because I felt that the people in my unit and the leadership were there just to avoid duty, and I just wasn't doing anything. I was sitting around wasting away within the walls of that tiny room in the dilapidated old building across from Mologne House. I had no motivation to be there and carry on this charade that I was still in the Army. I wasn't. I could no longer be an infantry soldier. That had been my purpose and my role within this organization. It was now completely impossible for me to fill that role. What motivated me now was back in Alabama. I had Colston and I had Tracy and I was needed back home.

When anyone leaves the military, whether it's because of injury, retirement, or they've fulfilled the obligation listed in their contract, every outgoing veteran receives a DD 214 form.

This is a certificate of release or discharge from active duty and it is the proof you have that you are in fact a veteran. It's basically a final report card for leaving your service branch. It lists all of the schools attended and awards won, and documents all the accomplishments achieved while serving in the U.S. military. I went in to see my platoon sergeant and he handed me my DD 214.

"Galloway, check this. It's your DD 214. Make sure it's correct," he said gruffly. I looked at it and there was nothing there. None of the schools I went to were listed. None of the training I received. None of the awards I was given. If anyone were to look at this, it looked like I lost my arm and leg during basic training. I looked up and asked, "What if it's wrong?"

"Well, we'd have to send it on up to Fort Campbell, find all the paperwork that's missing, get it corrected. You know, it takes some time," he replied.

That's all I needed to hear. "Looks good to me," I said and handed it back to him. I had already decided I was getting out of there. I was leaving. I approved it so that it was officially correct. I didn't care what was on the form. I just wanted to leave. I wasn't thinking about how it would affect my future. All I wanted was to go home.

I hung around a few more weeks before I decided, *Okay, enough. Time to go home.* The only person I told I was leaving was my physical therapist, Bob. I felt obliged to talk to him and to thank him. I never went to our appointments but I appreciated him nonetheless.

"Hey, Bob, I'm going home. I'm done here."

"Wow! That was quick," he said.

"Yeah, I am ready to go home," I replied.

"Noah, look, I wouldn't tell anybody else this. Everyone works differently. I actually think you improved faster and better because you did everything on your own. You're a strong walker. You've done very well."

I thanked him sincerely and told him that really meant a lot coming from him. I went back to my room, packed up all my stuff, and went to turn my key in back at the Mologne House. Before I left I took the elevator up to the second floor, and walked to room 224, the room where my parents stayed and then where I stayed for a long time. I walked up to the door and looked at the number. Next to every door of every room there was a gold-colored, oval-shaped plaque with red trim and red lettering for the room number. My eyes darted around quickly to see if anyone was in the hall and then I reached up and yanked that number plate right off the wall. I shoved it in my backpack and walked out. I calmly took the elevator down and walked out of the parking lot. I jumped in my Jeep and drove home.

As soon as I got home Tracy and I started looking at houses. We hired a real estate agent and we just about wore this guy out. We looked at house after house after house. We probably hit five or six a day. We knew just what we were looking for and finally we found it. We fell in love with a house in a quiet little cul-de-sac in Alabaster, a small town just outside Birmingham. It was on a one-acre lot, had a fenced-in yard, three bedrooms, two bathrooms, and a two-car garage. It was our little slice of the American dream. I bought the house and Tracy and I picked out new furniture to furnish it.

Right after I moved into the house I got a phone call from my platoon sergeant at Walter Reed.

"Galloway, where are you? You haven't been at formations!" he barked.

"No, I haven't. I'm in Alabama," I said flatly.

"What are you doing in Alabama?" he asked.

"I live here."

"You live there? You haven't out-processed! You haven't done anything. There is paperwork you have to do. There is protocol." He sounded exasperated.

"Figure it out. I just bought a house. I'm good." And I hung up the phone, because I didn't care. I went on about my life. And about a week later I get a phone call from Staff Sergeant Whoever. He said, "Sergeant Galloway, they put me in charge of your out-processing so I could take care of all of that and so you won't have to come back up here." And I said, "Sounds good to me, man. Appreciate it." And I hung up the phone. And that's how I got out of the Army.

PART TWO
CHALLENGES

———

▬▬▬▬

CHAPTER 8

A Life Begins;
A Marriage Ends

(2004–2005)

I RETURNED HOME from my first deployment Iraq in February 2004. It's a cliché to say war changes you, but it changed me. This was most obvious in my marriage. My focus had shifted. For most of my relationship I did whatever Brandi wanted. I deferred to her. Things started to shift on 9/11, when, despite her protests, I put my foot down and flat out told her I was enlisting.

She wasn't happy about this and she didn't understand. She didn't come from a military family like I did. 9/11 didn't affect her as it had affected me. She couldn't understand that sense of duty, that call to action that I had felt. But reluctantly she supported me in the end. And during my time in basic training we did get married. We were so young, probably too young to make that kind of decision but at the time I loved her. And it seemed like the right decision to make sure she was secure before I went to war.

It was during that year in Iraq that I found a real purpose. I went from really enjoying being in the military to being obsessed with it. I left Fort Campbell married to Brandi and I came home married to my job and to the military. She was living in this world where she had to share me. And eventually it went from sharing me to losing me.

While I was in Iraq my company wasn't living in a camp where we had access to phones all the time. People sent us prepaid calling cards, but we didn't really have any use for them. Guys who lived in camps benefited from that, but since we were living in abandoned buildings and banks, our resource to call home was an Iraqi with a satellite phone. We had to pay him three dollars a minute for use of his phone. Because of this, our phone access was limited and sporadic. So I would call Brandi every so often, but our conversations were all pretty superficial. I'd ask how she was, she'd ask how I was. I asked how the house was. Nothing was in depth or emotional. I didn't have the time for that. The other thing was, it wasn't occurring to me to call her all that much. I was so wrapped up in my life as a soldier that she just didn't cross my mind often. Our relationship was nothing like it was when I was in basic training where I broke the rules to call her as often as possible.

I didn't go home at Christmas and I lied about why. I had the option to go for two weeks' leave, but I turned it down. I didn't want to lose the edge I had in Iraq and I just didn't miss her. That sounds horrible but it's the truth. My purpose was now serving my country, fighting the enemy. Things between Brandi and me were strained at best.

When I got home, Brandi thought I was distant. She thought it was because of the war. She thought maybe I had PTSD or something. It wasn't anything like that. I just didn't feel connected to her. I only thought about wanting to go back. At first I thought I was going right back. That was the original plan. The 101st was supposed to return immediately. But then due to some restructuring and the addition of a fourth brigade they decided that, no, the 101st wouldn't go back until the fall of 2005.

Brandi and I struggled with our marriage, but it was obvious we were falling apart as a couple. That was probably clear to me even from as far away as Iraq, but I did try to make it better. One day I suggested marriage counseling. Initially Brandi agreed. I took advantage of the fact that the military has a program called Military OneSource. It's basically one-stop shopping for all the help you could need from moving, to retirement, to marriage counseling, as it turns out. So I called one day and asked to be set up with a marriage counselor. The morning of our appointment Brandi decided she didn't want to go. She didn't give much detail other than to say, "I'm not going." Annoyed, I said, "Well shit. I'm going."

I arrived and sat down in a chair across the counselor. He looked at the empty chair next to me and started flipping through the paperwork on his clipboard. Finally he looked up and asked, "I have down that you're here for marriage counseling?"

"Yes, sir, I am," I answered matter-of-factly. Again he looked at the empty seat next to me and then back at me.

And then, in a really deadpan tone, he said, "Huh. Seems like things are going well." We both laughed and then he said, "Well, you're here, so let's talk." I agreed, so we started talking. I stayed the full hour. Right around the end of the session he said, "Noah, I think you have ADD. I'd like to test you. Is that okay?"

I said that was fine and I took his test. He told me to come back in a few days. He set up my next appointment and said we could talk some more. I told him I was looking forward to it.

I walked in the door at home and Brandi asked, "Well? How did it go?"

"It was good. He thinks I have ADD, so I took this test," I said.

Brandi absolutely blew up at me.

"Everything is about you. It's always all about Noah!"

"I went to marriage counseling by myself. Who else is it going to be about?" I replied. I thought, *I was making the effort and she didn't bother. Why was she mad?*

I did go back to the doctor and he said, "Noah, I knew you had ADD when you walked in the room. I just didn't know how bad it was." He continued: "I gave you this test and the average person scores around a thirty. People with ADD score fifty or sixty. You're in the eighty range. You've got it bad." He said, "I fear that may be part of the problem in your marriage. I would suggest possibly getting on medication." I said, "Huh, let me get back to you." And I left knowing I wasn't going to follow up on that. I was totally focused on fitness and didn't like the idea of putting chemicals in my body.

Despite the counseling debacle, Brandi and I did try to make it work. We saw brief flickers of familiar excitement and read too much hope into them. We were still very young so we didn't know any better. I settled back as best I could into life at Fort Campbell. Brandi and I made some new friends and started going out again as a couple. We were behaving more like young married people. We enjoyed nightlife again and were having fun.

We got a puppy—a German shepherd named Super Dave Aloysius Galloway. We just called him Dave for short. He became part of our family. And then came the news that the family was about to get bigger. Brandi was pregnant. We thought maybe we were on the right track again.

While I was away Brandi had spent most of her time in Alabama with her family. Now that I was home she had come back to Fort Campbell and had gotten her job back at the day-care center. We weren't close enough to the due date yet to be worried about her working full-time, but she was pregnant enough to be uncomfortable and to tire easily. I was a little concerned when one night she came home saying she'd had contractions all day. But she assured me it was too early. Those were just false contractions. That's normal, she told me. She reassured me that all was well, so I went to work.

Shortly after I got to work Brandi called and said, "I think I need to go to the doctor."

"Are you sure?" I asked.

"Yes," she said definitively.

I told her I would be right there and went to my platoon sergeant to let him know what was going on. He told me to go ahead and keep him updated. I headed back home and picked up Brandi. When we got to the doctor's office, the nurses took their time. No one seemed panicked. Everything seemed normal and low-key until they began to examine her. Then the mood changed instantly, and things started to move really quickly. I nervously asked what was going on. One of the nurses shouted, "She's five centimeters!"

"What does that mean?" I asked.

"That means the baby is coming."

I knew this shouldn't be happening yet. The baby wasn't due for another six weeks. I was worried but focused hard on remaining calm for Brandi and the baby. The team started pumping her full of magnesium to try to stop the baby from coming. We were there all day long. Both her parents and my parents joined us at the hospital.

Finally, a doctor came in and said, "Look, we can't stop the baby from coming. We're going to start him on steroids, because the last things to form are the lungs, and this should help the lungs to form. We're not set up to deal with a premature baby here. So the ambulance is going to take you to another hospital."

The ambulance arrived and they helped Brandi inside through the back doors. A paramedic was in back with her, monitoring all of her and the baby's vital signs.

I hopped in the front seat and started talking to the driver. I don't know if I was suppressing my anxiety, but this was how I was dealing with it. I asked all kinds of questions not related to our situation and yammered on like we were on a Sunday drive. One interesting fact I learned is that ambulances have speed restrictions. I think they are allowed at maximum to ride at fifteen miles over the designated speed limit, and that's all.

Meanwhile, Brandi was in the back not very amused by my idle chatter, as she was in pain, in labor, and panicking because our baby was not supposed to be arriving anytime soon. When we arrived at the better-equipped hospital the paramedic said, "Yeah, this baby is coming now. I felt him drop. I was getting worried I might have to deliver that baby en route in the ambulance."

A team of doctors and nurses stood at attention for us outside the doors as the ambulance pulled up. They wheeled Brandi through the automatic doors of our second hospital of the day. We were rushed straight into a room. No stopping for paperwork or introductions. A doctor came in and a nurse started prepping everything for delivery. I just stood there feeling a little awkward. I wasn't sure what I should be doing or where I should be standing. I looked around and saw a table full of shiny surgical instruments and accidentally bumped into it. The shiny instruments all noisily tumbled to the floor. *Clang, clang, clang.* The nurses looked pissed. I was trying not to laugh at my clumsiness as they scrambled to pick up the now-unusable instruments and roll in a new tray. One of the nurses turned to face me and said, sternly, "Don't touch any of this. This is all sterile."

Next they took Brandi's finger and put ink on it to take her fingerprint. They handed me an alcohol wipe and told me to wipe the ink off her finger. I did as I was told. I didn't want to give the nurses any more reason to be mad at me. I'd caused enough trouble and we had more serious matters to deal with. Brandi turned to the nurse and asked, "What about my epidural?"

The nurse patted her on the arm and said, "Honey, we're past that."

Brandi turned and gave me a look that suggested if she could stand up on her own, she'd murder that nurse right there in that room.

The doctor walked in and didn't waste time with formalities. He sat down on a stool and glided it right up to Brandi's crotch.

"All right, Mrs. Galloway, what kind of baby are we having today?" he asked from down below.

But before we could muster up an answer another nurse popped her head in and said, "Doctor, the woman next door is having her baby. Right now."

He looked up, smiled, and told us he'll be right back. He pulled off his rubber gloves, tossed them in the trash, and walked out. Brandi and I tried to remain calm until he returned a little while later. He snapped on a new pair of rubber gloves, sat back down on his stool, and slid into position. "Okay. Let's do this for real. What are we having? A boy or a girl?" he asked.

"You know, we don't know. They sent us to do an ultrasound too soon and we couldn't tell," I answered.

The doctor looked up at us and said, "Well, I'm usually a pretty good judge. So give me a minute and I'll tell you what it is." He grinned and told me to join him on the business end.

From there things happened pretty quickly. I watched my baby's head crown in complete awe. I have always been fascinated by how things work and here I was getting a front seat on the miracle of life. And to top it off, it was my miracle of life. My baby. While I was down there getting a life science lesson, Brandi was pushing and screaming and hollering. I leaned into her and said, "Hey, I did my job and wiped the ink off your finger. All you gotta do is deliver this baby." I saw that death threat look again and decided it would be best if I went down to join the doctor.

And then, just like that, right after the head crowned, the baby just fell out. *Swoosh!* Thankfully he fell right into the doctor's hands. The doctor flopped our baby down right on top of Brandi and said, "Don't know for sure, but looks like a boy to me!"

It was official. I was a dad. We had a baby boy. We were so happy and he was so adorable. Shortly after, my buddies came to the hospital and we stood outside the glass looking into the nursery. I proudly pointed out my boy. And because I was there with my buddies and we assumed that glass was pretty thick, we were making off-color guy jokes. I said, "I'm going to get him a tattoo now and it will get bigger so he'll just grow into it. That will save him a bunch of money down the road." We all chuckled. And then there was another joke about his future sex life. That was when the nurses inside the glass baby aquarium looked up. They all glared at us disapprovingly. "Oh shit! They can hear us," I said, as we all scattered.

One of the nurses had said, "The first twenty-four hours is like the honeymoon stage. Everything seems fine. And if something is going to go wrong, it's going to happen toward the end of that twenty-four hours." As it got later on that first night, I pulled two chairs together to form a makeshift cot. Brandi and I were both exhausted, so we fell asleep quickly. Then suddenly the door to our room flew open and the fluorescent light from the hallway flooded in. The nurses were all talking at once at what seemed like ninety miles an hour. I was half-asleep and having trouble following what they were saying.

We finally heard, "Y'all are going to Nashville. You're being sent to Children's Hospital in Nashville. There are some issues with the baby."

She then led me out into the hallway and pulled an X ray out of a large envelope. She held it up against the light and said, "You see this spot right here in his stomach?" I nodded as I looked at the little black spot. She continued: "Food is not going through the intestines right here. He's spitting up dangerous bile that normally a newborn poops. Nothing is getting past that spot. He spits it all up. Something has to be done to fix this." I was completely stunned but managed to say, "Okay." Then she said, "He can't leave this hospital until we have a name for the birth certificate. What's his name?"

We didn't have a name. We had thought we had all the time in the world to talk names. He was so early we didn't even know he'd be a he. I walked back into the room and explained to Brandi what was going on and that we needed a name, fast. Our parents came into the room to try to help. My mom kept saying, "Make him a junior. Noah Matthew Jr." I said no. I had no desire to make him a junior. Brandi's parents were suggesting names, too, that we didn't like. And then my mom said, "What about Colston? It's your dad's middle name and his dad's middle name. And somewhere down the line it was a last name. You can give him your middle name, Matthew." I liked it. I looked at Brandi and repeated it: "Colston Matthew." Her parents were immediately opposed to it. "If you call him that, we're calling him something else. We will give him a nickname."

I turned to Brandi and said, "He's our baby. We'll call him whatever the hell we want. I like Colston. Do you?" She said, "Yes. I do like Colston." I said, "All right." I turned to the nurse and said, "His name is Colston Matthew Galloway." The nurse filled out the birth certificate and the next thing I knew we were being rushed down to the Children's Hospital in Nashville in another ambulance.

There we met Dr. Yang, our surgeon. Dr. Yang had olive skin and jet-black hair that he slicked straight back. He looked young but wore big, clunky-looking glasses, which made him look older and more serious. His youth didn't bother me, because right away he struck me as intelligent and confident, exactly what you want in someone who is going to save your kid's life.

Dr. Yang explained to us that it is not uncommon for a small piece of intestine to die. He would be going in and cutting out that piece of intestine, then sewing the intestines back together. He assured us it would be easy to do.

"It's been a long night and morning for you. Go to the cafeteria. By the time you eat, we should be done," he said. We said okay and kissed our son before they whisked him off to surgery. We headed down to the cafeteria.

As soon as we got there they called us back upstairs. Our parents had also made the drive to Nashville, so they were there with us, too. Dr. Yang came back in and said, "I want to talk to the parents alone."

Brandi and I left our parents and followed Dr. Yang down a dimly lit hallway into another room. Dr. Yang started drawing on the white dry-erase board attached to the back wall. As he scribbled unidentifiable objects on the whiteboard he explained that Colston's small intestines had twisted up on themselves. By the time they opened him up in surgery, circulation had been cut off for so long that 75 percent of his small intestines had died. He continued drawing to show us just how his intestines were swollen and where the blockage was and what was causing Colston to spit up everything instead of passing it. To fix this problem they'd have to figure out how to make the intestines small enough to work food through them. Generally they cut them in half to make them smaller. He needed our permission to try a relatively new procedure on our boy. The surgery had been invented three years earlier by a doctor in Boston, where Dr. Yang served his internship.

The procedure was called a serial transverse enteroplasty, also known as STEP. He once again started scribbling across the whiteboard to explain. He said they would cut Colston's intestines in a zigzag pattern and in time it would stretch and Colston would be more likely to take full advantage of his small intestine. He then told us that only four kids had ever had this procedure, but he could perform it. After surgery, Colston would have a stomach tube, a central line to feed nutrients straight to his heart, and possibly a colostomy bag. But before they could try this procedure, they needed our permission. I looked at Brandi and she was completely frozen with fear. She said nothing. I stood up and I erased everything on the whiteboard. I redrew every symbol and talked out every step as I went.

"This zigzag pattern is so the intestines will stretch over time?" I asked.

"That's exactly it," he said.

I dropped down to my knees right in front of Brandi sitting in that chair. I grabbed her hands and said, "We don't have another option. We have to do this." She didn't say anything. She just nodded. I turned to Dr. Yang and said, "Go do it." Without a word, he left the room.

As we waited I managed to stay calm the whole time. I didn't cry. I didn't let myself. I had a job to do that day. I had to be the rock for my wife and my son. It wasn't until sometime later that Brandi told me how much that helped her. She said I was acting as if everything were fine and normal and that if I had not done that, she likely wouldn't have made it through those hours we waited, and those first few days in general. I did the best I could. I tried to point out the upside in everything we were dealing with. We were told that one of the obstacles later would be that he'd be restricted from certain kinds of food. So while we were sitting in the waiting room I said to her, "Brandi, so what? He will have to eat healthy for the rest of his life? That's not such a bad thing. He is going to grow up and be just as normal as other kids. In fact, he will probably be healthier than other kids because of this." Through her tears she was able to smile and nod.

When the surgery was over, they brought Colston into the Neonatal ICU complete with a shiny new stomach tube and central line, but no colostomy bag. So that was already a win. The NICU became our new home for the next three months.

I am very grateful that my chain of command treated my situation with the utmost kindness and consideration. Our battalion commander said I needed to be present for formation every morning, but then I could leave and go to the hospital. But the hospital in Nashville was forty-five minutes away from Fort Campbell, so my platoon sergeant said, "That's stupid. You stay there. Take care of your boy. We'll say that you are here." And that is what we did. Brandi and I created our own routine as well. I would stay in the room at night with Colston and part of the day while Brandi was with him all day. We had a room at the Ronald McDonald House as our home base for the entirety of Colston's hospital stay.

Dr. Yang would visit every day because he was waiting for Colston's first bowel movement. Every day he was a little more anxious than the day before.

"You tell me when he has a bowel movement," he said on every visit. It was a good week before Colston finally had a bowel movement. Baby's first milestone.

We learned that eating is a learned behavior. So because Colston had a feeding tube we made it a point to also feed him with a bottle. We didn't want him to just be fed through the tube because then he'd never learn how to eat properly.

Dr. Yang explained that Colston would probably have the stomach tube until he was about six years old. They hoped to remove the central line as quickly as possible because it was pumping medicine directly into his heart. We were waiting for his intestines to start absorbing and taking nutrients in naturally.

I noticed that there was a computer in the waiting room. This was 2005, so I didn't have a tiny computer with Google capabilities in my pocket just yet. I would sit in that waiting room on that computer for hours and just comb through dozens and dozens of articles online. I wanted to teach myself everything there was to learn about the small intestine.

Once, after one of my Google searches, I was standing in Colston's room and Dr. Yang came in. I said, "Dr. Yang, there are three parts of the intestines, right?" He looked surprised but answered, "Yes, there are."

I continued. "Which part of the small intestine did Colston lose the most of?"

"He lost all of the ileum and part of the jejunum," he replied.

"Huh. He lost all of the ileum? Isn't that the part that absorbs all of the nutrients?" I asked.

He reluctantly answered yes.

"Are we just hoping that the body will just form a new ileum?"

"Yes, that's what we're hoping."

"All right, just wanted to make sure we were on the same page," I said.

It was a terrifying thing to realize that this tiny baby had completely lost a part of his body that we could only hope his body would regenerate. I understood why Dr. Yang didn't spell it out like that to us. Why freak out the parents over something they can't control?

Colston's case garnered some attention. The surgery had only been done on four other kids with short bowel syndrome before and at most they had lost 25 percent of their small intestines. Colston had lost 75 percent. And he was thriving. Naturally people wanted to hear about it, so the hospital hosted a few press conferences. Dr. Yang and his miracle patient were in the spotlight. This was funny to watch because when we met Dr. Yang he was a pretty nerdy-looking guy with slicked-back hair and oversize glasses. He was also really nervous in front of the camera and sweated a lot. But as time went on and he got more and more press conferences under his belt, he sweated less and he even was rocking a little bit of swagger. He'd either gotten Lasik or contact lenses, because gone were those thick, Coke-bottle glasses. He also had a new hairstyle. It was like watching a butterfly coming out of his cocoon.

As Colston improved day by day, Brandi and I were deteriorating. Our families came in and out of town to help us, but for the most part it was just the two of us. And we fought about everything. We were starting to unravel. I don't even know what we were fighting about most of the time. We were staying in the Ronald McDonald House and the walls to those rooms are paper thin. We didn't want to disturb the other families so instead of screaming we were whispering. We were whispering our screams at each other. One night it was just too much for me to deal with within those quiet walls. I grabbed the keys and whisper-snapped, "I'm going outside."

I headed to the door and had my hand on the doorknob when she said, "Don't you leave with that car." We only had one at the time. I said, "I ain't leaving. I'm just going outside." Standing just inside the door with her arms crossed over her chest she said, "Well, then you can leave the keys here." I threw them down on the other side of the hallway and turned and walked out. I knew I wasn't leaving. But I knew I had to take a moment to myself. We were coming unglued. But we needed to focus all of our energy on Colston.

Three months later we finally got to go home with our son. A machine was delivered to the house that would hook up to his stomach tube and constantly run formula through it. Colston needed a steady stream of food to make sure he was getting the proper nutrients, because he was constantly pooping. A nurse came to deliver all the equipment and showed Brandi how to clean and rebandage the central line that was inserted on the left side of his chest near his armpit. I remember she told Brandi, "Look, you want to prevent an infection but don't overthink it. He's going to end up with an infection. Over time it's going to happen. But you're going to do your best to prevent it by keeping it clean, changing the bandage, but don't feel bad. Don't feel like you failed if he does get an infection because nine times out of ten, everyone does."

While the nurse showed Brandi how to clean the central line, I figured out the machine. I hit START and the machine began to pump formula into my child. When the nurse felt confident that Brandi understood her instructions, she left. As soon as she left Brandi broke down crying. "I can't do this. This is going to be so hard," she wailed.

I sat her down and scooped up her hands in mine. I looked her in the eyes and assured her, "Everything will be fine. Colston will be just fine! You will be great with the bandages and I will deal with the stomach tube. Everything is going to be fine." I was convincing but I would be lying to say I wasn't terrified myself. That first night home was rough. Suddenly there were no nurses or doctors around. It was just us.

We had to learn to be new parents, but we had the added responsibility of being parents to a delicate and sick child. It was a lot to take in. Slowly but surely we got the hang of things.

I figured out that the trick to getting the baby to sleep all night was to make sure he had a full stomach. Now, when you have a child with a stomach tube, you can make sure he's full. I would pour his formula into him and I would fill him all the way up. Then I hooked the machine up and hit START. He slept through the night every night. He was never a problem because he was always full. I made sure of that. I gave him the bottle before because we still wanted to reinforce that sucking behavior. But then I'd just fill him up.

When we left the house with Colston, we could disconnect the stomach tube, which basically left this hole in his stomach. A plastic piece slid in and we injected a little fluid so it made a bubble on the inside and held it in place. The tube could be disconnected, and the hole closed up, and then we could leave the house.

We could also disconnect the central line and just an inch or so of tubing would be hanging off Colston. We could close that up and go. If we were going to be away from home for more than a couple of hours we had a backpack and a little portable machine in it that pumped the medicine through it. We could wear the backpack or throw it in the bottom of the stroller and hook it up to him wherever we went. If we went back home to Alabama or somewhere for a few days we'd have to pack the big machine. But if we were just going to be out and about for the day, the backpack did the trick. We adapted quickly to Colston's unique needs.

We visited my family in Alabama one time for a weekend. We stayed at my grandmother's house and my aunts were in town as well. Everyone wanted to see Baby Colston. One night of the visit my aunt LuAnn said, "Y'all go to bed. We will take care of Colston. Don't worry about it. I'll stay with him."

Brandi and I were so grateful. We were exhausted. We headed to bed but it wasn't long before Brandi shook me awake. "Colston's stomach tube popped out," she said with panic in her voice.

That had never happened before! It just popped out and everything inside him was leaking out. But LuAnn didn't freak out. She was cool and calm and she and Brandi were able to put the tube back in and solve the problem.

Brandi and I were adjusting to life with a baby and Colston was growing and improving. Everything seemed to be going well. We went down to Nashville once a week for an appointment at the children's hospital. By this point it had also come down the chain of command that I would not be returning to Iraq with the company. I had missed a lot of training. While I was taking care of Colston my company had gone to the National Training Center at Fort Irwin in California. I obviously couldn't have joined them. So I wasn't going to be deployed with them this time. I was fine with that. My son came first. While they were out west, I stayed at post and was in charge of the new privates when they arrived. I took care of getting them situated. It was a good job to have in a time when I needed to be close to home and able to go take care of Colston if something came up.

Brandi was great with Colston but it was still a lot of stress on her. She needed to have time to take breaks, so we got to the point where she was with him during the day every day while I was at work. At night she'd go out and drink with her friends and I would stay home with him. We were both good parents, but we were on different shifts. We were parents but not spouses.

One day I saw that *The Notebook* was out on DVD so I bought it. I will fully admit to enjoying a good chick flick every now and again. I didn't really think Brandi would stay home to watch with me, so I scooped up Colston in my lap and turned it on. I knew it was sad and I prepared myself for what I thought was the sad part. I had my wall up in front of my emotions and knew this movie wasn't going to get me. So the sad part came and I didn't tear up, and I think, *I've beaten Nicholas Sparks in this battle*, and I relaxed. Then out of nowhere the movie hit me with another sad part. I was not expecting that. I thought to myself, *Oh no, I am going to ugly cry*. I sat Colston down in his bouncy chair and walked out of the room. I thought he was too young to see his father crying. And while I did buy the movie because I wanted to see it, I couldn't ignore the fact that I was sitting there watching a love story while there was just no love left in my house.

At one of Colston's regular weekly checkups in Nashville they told us that things were going great. So great that they said they could take out the central line and the stomach tube. This was huge news. We didn't think either would happen when he was only seven months old. And we certainly didn't expect that he would be able to get rid of both of them at the same time. Miraculously, just as Dr. Yang had hoped, a new ileum had formed. I was in the room with Colston for the removal. In fact, I held him. I held his left arm up and held his legs when they removed the central line and basically cut the skin that had grown around it. He was screaming and hollering as they took it out and bandaged him up, but then when it was over, he just stopped crying. There was no memory of the pain. It was something I never forgot.

After the tubes came out, I started to feel that Colston would be all right and that he didn't need me as badly now, that he would continue to improve and develop like a normal child. My focus shifted back to my duty as a soldier. I felt compelled to rejoin my company on our second deployment. The family crisis was over and I had a job to do. It was also clear that aside from Colston, I had no reason to stay. Brandi and I were definitely hanging on by a very thin thread. In fact, when I told her that I wanted to go back to Iraq with the company she wasn't happy about it, but I think there was a part of her that just felt, *Sure, go. I don't care.* She didn't fight it. I started to push at work to get back on that deployment. When I was granted permission to deploy I decided I needed to prepare for the "what-ifs." Behind Brandi's back I went to see a lawyer about divorce.

I told the lawyer about what was happening in my marriage. When he realized that I was going to be deployed, he asked, "Does she know you're seeing a lawyer?"

"No," I said.

"Well then, don't say anything about it. Because if you try to divorce her right now, all she has to do is contest it and she'll delay it. You'll go to Iraq, she'll have full control of your money, knowing that you're leaving her and she can do whatever she wants with your money. So I would advise you to just keep your mouth shut, deploy, come home, and then get a divorce," he said.

He then explained that there were things that I could and should do before I left. I made sure that Colston was taken care of no matter what, should something happen to me. I also made my mother my power of attorney. She was the one who had the right to make medical decisions for me now. Brandi still had the power to take care of Colston and she'd be provided for to do that. But that was it.

I didn't file any sort of divorce papers before I left, but the marriage was over. Brandi knew it and I knew it. There was just no connection, and it caused so much tension in the house that we found a reason to fight about everything. So I made sure I was gone during the day, and she'd go out in the evening. But when we had to be around each other on the weekends or when I wasn't working, we just fought.

I don't even think I realized it at the time, that this was also about choosing my job over her. I hadn't come to that conclusion yet, but I really was married to the military instead of Brandi. She didn't understand, but then again, I don't know how she could have. I am not good at balancing different areas of my life.

Maybe this is how the ADD that doctor had told me about was impacting my life. I could only concentrate on one thing in my life at a time. All Brandi said about my return to Iraq was a weak protest. "Really? With all that Colston's been through?" I just said, "He's better now so now I have a job to do." I think I also saw deployment as a way to hit the pause button. I could always argue that this is my job, this is what I do for a living. But this time I was also just in need of a break. And it wasn't from Colston.

CHAPTER 9

Return to Combat

(September 2005)

I BOARDED THE PLANE and found my seat. With my rucksack beside me I secured my seat belt and settled in for the long flight overseas. I thought about how different this felt, this second deployment. The farewells in the parking lot at Fort Campbell were the same and yet entirely different. We were in the same place; it was early morning again. My parents were there again and so was Brandi. Just like before. Only I wasn't emotional at all. I felt like I was trying to keep everyone else calm. I kept saying, "I'll be back. This is no big deal." I was very much ready to get back to doing my job.

Brandi was emotional and crying and I just didn't feel any of it. Only something was different: Colston. Colston was there and I was feeling a huge amount of emotion about leaving him. But I didn't express it. I kept telling myself that I was doing this for him. I was pursuing a way of life that would help shape him, by example, into a man one day. Only later would I also think, *I hope he never experiences things like this.* But leaving him rattled me in a way I hadn't felt before. I had his picture with me and carried it every single day.

* * *

I was jostled awake on a dark plane somewhere in the air over the Atlantic. The first time I had made this flight I was giddy about the unknown adventures that awaited me on the battlefield. I spent the flight chatting away with the flight attendants and other soldiers. Now, staring at the headrest of the seat in front of me, I was aware of how much quieter this flight was. We all knew the seriousness of the tasks that awaited us on the ground. But for me, I also felt heavier. Yes, I wanted to be here. Yes, I knew this is where I belonged. I was built to be a soldier and to defend the world and my country from the enemy. I rubbed my thumb over the picture of Colston I had in my hand. I looked at my sweet baby's face in that small photograph and I knew that everything I did from here on out mattered more than anything that had come before.

When we landed in Kuwait, it looked completely different from how we had left it in 2004. When we returned to the first camp, our holdover zone until we could get back into Iraq, gone were the tents I'd slept in that first night. Now there were aluminum Quonset huts that looked like half cylinders stuck in the ground. Inside were rows and rows of beds.

Kuwait itself was different. It had become Americanized, with fast-food joints from Burger King to Pizza Hut. We also didn't have to carry our weapons or our gas masks when walking around town anymore. There was no longer a threat of attack here.

After a few days in Kuwait, we boarded large military planes, C-130s. These are pretty much cargo planes but they have narrow bench seats that line the walls and the inside. We all piled in and headed into Iraq at night. As we approached Baghdad the plane had to zig and zag, up and down, and maneuver every which way to deter anyone from trying to shoot the plane down.

We landed at Camp Victory, just outside Baghdad. It was huge and ridiculously nice. There was everything you could ever want in a resort. It was far nicer than Ft. Campbell. The people stationed at that camp had nothing to worry about.

It was so big that it had an area known as the Green Zone because mortars and missiles couldn't reach it. It was a totally safe, threat-free area in the middle of a war zone. There was a basketball court and guys were out playing a casual game of pickup. I even remember seeing a stage with stadium seating.

The camp felt like a little town. There was even a bus stop and a bus that would take us to the PX. I took advantage of that to get some last-minute stuff I wanted to take with me. A PX is like a miniature Wal-Mart. You can buy just about anything there, from socks and uniforms to Pringles and beef jerky. And that's not all. There was a display of Oakley sunglasses and there was an area where you could look through a catalog and purchase a Harley-Davidson or a Chevrolet truck, tax free. It was there primarily for use by the U.S. military but British soldiers were welcome there also. It was a huge superstore and a busy hub on camp. It was so nice that walking into one basically felt like being back in the

States. I can see where a lot of guys would feel comforted by that. But all I wanted was to get the hell out of there. I was ready to push out of that camp. This wasn't the real Iraq. That's what I wanted. I felt ready to do my job and I couldn't wait to leave.

We spent about a week at the luxurious camp before we finally headed out to a tiny outpost. From there we were loaded into Humvees and sent to our designated area: a potato storage building U.S. forces had previously taken under control. What we found there was shocking. Security surrounding the building was a joke. But that was nothing compared to what we found when we walked through the door. The stench hit you in the face. These guys were living in utter filth. And I'm not talking about, well, this is a war zone so you'd expect there to be poor living conditions. No, I'm talking about pure, lazy-man-created filth. There were actually bottles full of urine all over the floor. Guys were pissing in bottles and then just leaving them around the room haphazardly.

I'm embarrassed to have to say that the men living in this squalor were part of a National Guard unit. Let me say that I have the utmost respect for people who work full-time jobs and then also serve in the National Guard. That means they are willing to put the uniform on when necessary and that is a big sacrifice for country. But the National Guard is a quick reaction force. That means it was created in order to respond if something happens or a need arises in a state. For example, if a tornado wipes out half of Alabama, the Alabama National Guard is called into action to help.

War is a completely different situation. When we are fighting a war on foreign soil, one weekend a month, two weeks a year in total just won't cut it. I also understand that many retired military who did serve full-time and have more in-depth training do come back and join the National Guard. However, on the whole, it's people who train one weekend a month. I am not belittling what they are capable of and how they do help those in need, but I was a soldier full-time. It's all I thought about. I had basic training alone for sixteen weeks. It's just a different level of training. It's like expecting someone who interned at a law firm for a summer to be able to jump in as lead defense attorney and win a murder trial. The proof is what happened to these troops when someone made the mistake of saying, "Let's put the National Guard in combat."

At first, they were just sitting in camps. That was fine. But they shouldn't have been pushed out into a war zone. The group we found that day in a potato warehouse in Yusafiah, southwest of Baghdad, was there to relieve a unit of marines who had stabilized the area and were moving on. The Guardsmen were supposed to keep it stable. Instead they just sat there for three months. When we arrived they started telling my platoon leader, Jerry Eidson, things like, "Oh, we don't go down that road," or "We don't use this road anymore." When Jerry asked why not, the answer was, "Because we hit a roadside bomb there." One of the guys even said, "Hey, just sit here until your time is up."

As a result of their lack of action, the entire surrounding area was wired and ready to blow. All the progress the marines had made before these guys showed up was lost. The enemy had full control of the area. We had to clean up the mess they made. This set everything into motion for our company and a dangerous deployment. We were no longer fighting the enemy. We were fighting just to survive.

This was only part of the problem. The other part was poor leadership. The war had taken its toll and things were very different on this second deployment. The worst part for me was our battalion commander, whom we called Colonel Punk and which pretty much sums up my sentiment about the man. He was a big, broad-shouldered fellow, probably about six foot three, with a bald head and a face only a mother could love. He didn't make up for it with his personality, either. He was loud, rude, and obnoxious. It seems to me that Punk was trying so hard to puff up his own chest and come off as a badass that he undermined and micromanaged all of the commanders of our battalion. This false bravado was conveyed at such a level that I could only assume he was overcompensating for something.

Unfortunately, Bravo company's commander, my company commander, wasn't immune from Punk's raging ego. Captain Goodwin was assigned to us right before we deployed. He was one of those National Guard guys. And I felt bad for him. Purely because there was a screwup with his paperwork, he ended up with us in a war zone, and Goodwin was not prepared for the situation into which he had been thrown.

Because of this, Captain Goodwin was a weak leader, unsure of himself. Punk took full advantage of this and made Goodwin the target for much of his barrage of criticism. This deeply affected Captain Goodwin and made it almost impossible for him to lead us as company commander. He didn't stand up for us when Punk would make ridiculous decisions like the one to have us put a Humvee in every intersection after a roadside bomb went off there. He thought if we sat there long enough, surely the enemy would return and we could catch them. It was a ridiculous waste of resources, not to mention extremely dangerous, to have us park in an intersection and be sitting ducks.

On one of these missions we were in an intersection next to a vacant building. Our platoon set up camp inside as we rotated out guys to man the Humvee. We were just sitting around in the dirt in this building and were there a long time, so we eventually got hungry. We started to snack on MREs (military "Meals, Ready to Eat") we had in our packs. They were left over from the first deployment because no one ate MREs anymore. People were living in luxurious camps and eating meals prepared for them by kitchen staff. They had no need for MREs when they could have steak and lobster on Thursday nights. Well, we didn't have access to that. We weren't living in those camps. We were living in the midst of a war zone twenty-four hours a day, seven days a week. So there we were with these old MREs that had been in extreme cold and then extreme heat a few times over. I opened mine up and squeezed cheese onto a cracker. The cheese was green. I scraped the putrid green cheese, the color of baby vomit, off and ate the cracker. I was hungry and had no other options. The other guys ate the expired MREs and started vomiting. Enough guys got sick that we were rushed some new kosher MREs. Yes, saved by the kosher meal option.

So we were dealing with Punk and his bogus ideas, but at the same time we also had to reclaim the area. Our company took over that potato factory, but there was also a bridge over the Euphrates River we had to worry about. One platoon was assigned to set up camp there while the rest of us were at the potato plant. We would rotate and each platoon spent thirty days at the bridge. But in order for that to be safe and successful, first we had to fortify both places. We spent a day putting metal stakes into the ground, running barbed wire around the perimeters, and cleaning up enough to make the area livable. First Platoon went to the bridge first and started fortifying it. After thirty days we rotated out to the bridge. We continued the previous platoon's efforts to fortify it and did everything we could to make it safe.

Roadside bombs were a new feature of this deployment. They hadn't been in use in 2003. At first the setup was the Iraqis would place a bomb and run a wire into the bushes that was attached to a detonator. They'd try to time it as we rolled through. But that was easy enough to handle. We learned to speed through so it was harder for them to hit the button. Often the bomb would explode just in front or just behind us. And whichever side it hit told us where there was someone in the bushes who had set it off. Our gunners would then spray the side of the road with bullets. Unlike the first deployment, when we were in highly populated cities, we were now out in farmland. There was much less of a chance of hitting an innocent bystander. If someone was in those bushes, there was no doubt that it was the insurgent who had just tried to blow us up.

But just as we adapted, so, too, did the enemy. They started using Motorola pagers. This way they could detonate the bomb from the other side of the road or in a building; from anywhere, really. We couldn't just shoot sporadically all around us. But we had an answer for that, too. A company designed an antenna for the military that went on top of our Humvees. It scrambled the signal from the pagers. This caused a delay in detonation and saved a lot of lives. But not all. We lost a couple of guys pretty early on. I missed sleep over it, but it was the new guys who'd never been deployed before who took it the hardest. The night after it happened, one of the guys came to talk to me. He knew we'd lost a guy I was close with, Rel Ravago, in our first deployment. He wanted to know how to deal with the loss. I talked him through it as best I could. Then there was another guy who wanted to talk. That night was a lot of talking and a lot of grieving. I didn't intentionally take on the role of counselor, but I had been through it before. It's not a club anybody wants to be a member of, but I was one. I did know how it felt. I was able to offer some insight. Or at least I tried. It was hard to relive the emotions I felt over losing Ravago. Talking my guys through their grief only brought painful memories to the surface I'd worked very hard to bury.

* * *

It was nearing Christmas 2003, and soon my first deployment would be over. Soon enough I would be heading back home to my wife after a year away. So much had changed for me in that time and I was aware of it. My behavior was different and so was my focus. When I was in basic training I had called Brandi every chance I got. I spent a lot of my time scheming about ways to sneak a call to her when I wasn't allowed to use the phone. I had lived for those stolen moments when I could hear her voice or her laugh on the other end of the line. But here I was, half a world away, and while it was much harder to call her, I wasn't thinking about it. I was drifting. I was falling more and more in love with my job and out of love with my wife. Next to war, everything else seemed secondary. So when we got word as the holidays were approaching that they were letting people take two weeks leave, I turned mine down. I called Brandi to tell her and I lied about it. I told her I was too low down the totem pole and hadn't been granted leave. I'd seen other guys go home and come back and their heads weren't in the game anymore. I didn't want to lose my edge. So I stayed.

Because most people did go home, there was a need to cover their positions. The sergeant major's driver took leave and so they were going to pick someone to fill in for those two weeks. This job is pretty cushy. You're not out doing patrols, you're living on a camp, and life is pretty good. They chose Rel Ravago. He was an awesome guy and loved by the whole company. We all agreed that he deserved this special assignment. He never complained. He always just did his job. So the company sent Ravago to aid the sergeant major for two weeks. It turns out this sergeant major was doing some things he shouldn't have. He made a poor decision to go somewhere he shouldn't and because it was something he wasn't supposed to be doing he didn't follow protocol. You were never supposed to go anywhere alone. There were supposed to be three Humvees at all times. On this particular night he went out with just his driver, Ravago. I don't know all the details, but what we do know is there was an ambush, and they were hit. They were dragged out of the vehicles, beaten, and killed, their bodies stripped of everything.

By the time any information reached us, it was too late. We had to secure the entire area and I stood just a couple of hundred yards away from the Humvee while Ravago's best friend was asked to formally identify the body. He walked back past me and he was sobbing. Everything changed for me then. I was overcome with anger. I was angry at the situation, angry at leadership. And I remember having this feeling that I wanted to cry, but I didn't let it out. I bottled it up. It was only later, while I was out on patrol, standing in the back of a truck manning a 240 Bravo machine gun, that I cried. I was alone so I felt safe to briefly let a few tears trickle down my face. This was the first casualty of war in my world. This was the first moment where the consequences of war became grimly real to me. As we approached our destination and I was no longer going to be alone, I wiped my tears with my sleeve, took a deep breath, and swallowed my grief deep inside, where it stayed.

Ravago's death came at a time when we as a military unit had become too relaxed. That was the one thing that was always preached at us: do not fall into complacency. But it was almost as if we felt we'd won the war, and it was over. But that wasn't true. We were still in danger. And I felt very much like Rel Ravago's death was a direct result of our military letting its guard down and taking our safety for granted.

I wasn't the only one. A lot of people were angry about his death. Unfortunately, the result was that guys became more aggressive. Here we were trying to restore peace and order, and to do that we had to win over the hearts and minds of the locals. But none of us wanted to try anymore. Suddenly if there was an opportunity to shoot or beat somebody up, we took it. We still observed the international rules of engagement, so we couldn't just shoot somebody at random without justification. Even the locals were very much aware of the rules of engagement. They were not scared if you pointed a weapon at them. If they didn't have a weapon on them, they knew they were safe. So we started carrying ax handles. Those we could use. We became just a bunch of hoodlums—we had this aggression and we figured out a way around the system.

We were in the city of Mosul to maintain order while the new police force was being established. The marketplace was a struggle. There was no order and it was difficult to walk through because the vendors all placed their carts wherever they pleased. They pulled their carts out in front of one another and onto the street. We were constantly correcting them. And this was at a time where our anger came out in an inappropriate way. If we told one of these guys to move his cart and he didn't, or he moved it back out into the street, we'd lose it. We'd destroy the cart. We were smashing cantaloupes all over the street. The guy at the next cart would see that and so he'd pull his cart back halfway, so we'd wreck that cart, too. We felt that we were being disrespected by the locals, and every day we were out looking for trouble. We were looking for someone to slip up and give us a reason to beat him up or destroy his cart.

I had gotten good at a new thuggish habit. I would be walking down the sidewalk and would casually step off the sidewalk right into traffic just so the driver would have to lock his brakes. This led to a habit of beating cars. I punched their hoods, their grilles, took off side-view mirrors. Twice I got hit by a car, but I knew how to roll over the hood and land safely.

One day I stepped out in front of a little Toyota truck and it hit me. I rolled onto my back, rolled over, and landed just by the driver's-side door. The man driving said pleadingly, "Sorry, mister, sorry, sorry." But without hesitation, I slammed my fist into his face. I hit him, his head wrap fell forward into his lap, and he was bleeding. I looked over into the passenger seat and there was a six-year-old boy sitting there. Terrified. And I felt like the biggest asshole. Within a split second I thought of how bad it would be to be six years old riding with my dad and witness someone disrespect him and punch him in the face. I grunted at the guy to get the fuck out of there and he sped off.

The next day I pulled guard duty on a roof. I sat up there looking out at the horizon, thinking about who I'd become and my behavior toward the merchants. And I thought about that little boy and his dad. I tried to rationalize that I was behaving that way because these people were disrespectful. But they really weren't, and even so, was it necessary to beat people up? The expression of that scared little boy really disturbed me. It shook me to my core. His father had done nothing. I caused it. It was all about giving myself a reason to hit somebody. I didn't realize it as it was happening but I guess it was triggered by Ravago's death. My aggression increased after his death, for sure. Maybe it was because I had buried my grief, but regardless, there is no excuse for that kind of behavior.

A couple of days later, I went on patrol with a different attitude. We walked by a group of men sitting at a plastic table outside a shop. They were sitting there drinking hot tea out of these tiny glasses. I walked by and said, "S'alam alacheim." They looked kind of irritated but replied, "Alacheim s'alam." I smiled at them. And then their whole demeanor changed. Their response went from one of forced respect to appreciation of a genuine act of kindness. They let their guard down—all because of a smile. It was a small but powerful gesture. From then on I found it much easier to work with the locals. There would still be moments

where aggression was necessary but there was no need to go looking for those. These people were on guard because we were causing violence. It doesn't always happen with a simple smile, but
I realized that it was up to us, up to me, to show them that we
were really there to help them. We were there to try to stop the
attacks and to defeat what was left of the enemy. The only way we
could do our job was to get information from the locals. We had
to make them feel respected in order to be respected in return.

Things started to change. I wasn't as angry anymore. That
one look from that one little boy shook me back to reality. My
anger over Ravago's death would still surface once in a while, but
for the most part I had learned to see things more clearly. I can't
help but think, this kid is nineteen years old now. What does he
think of Americans? What good did I do for his country? What
kind of chain reaction did I set in motion at that moment? And
what about all the other times when I did the same thing? How
many ripples of anger did I cause that became violent waves?

* * *

I struggled with leadership in my second deployment, but that
didn't apply to everyone—especially my platoon leader, Jerry Eidson. I had met Jerry just before deployment. He had been brought
into our platoon only a few months before. But right away I liked
him. He took the time to get to know me and seemed genuinely
concerned about Colston and my family. We started working out
together before we left and our friendship quickly grew. During
one of those pre-deployment workouts he asked me about Iraq
and about being in combat. This would be Jerry's first deploy-

ment and he was worried. I assured him that no matter what happened, I had his back. I would take care of him, and I meant it. So, because of that promise, and just because we got along so well, he and I were attached at the hip upon arriving in Iraq. If our platoon broke into smaller groups, we were almost always together.

We'd been in Iraq about a month and had lost our first few guys when we received some intel that the teenage boy responsible for their deaths was hiding in a particular house. Our mission was to raid and secure this house and find our suspect. This is the job infantry is intended to do and what I had done all the time in my first deployment. This made sense to me. Everyone was excited. Jerry was especially excited because he hadn't really gotten to use his infantry skills yet. In all honesty, Jerry was most excited because we were finally going to kick down some doors.

Proper procedure for invading a house is to take a four-man team and "stack" it outside the door. That means the men are essentially in a line—numbered one through four. Number four comes around to check that no one has booby-trapped the house. He nods to number one. Number one then leans back on number two, number two leans back on number three, number three then pushes back forward on number two, number two pushes back on number one, number one nods to number four, and number four kicks in the door. Number one runs in, followed by two, three, and four. Everyone makes sure that the room is clear and then everyone stacks back in place for the next door. This is the way you move strategically and stealthily through the house until all is secure and any targets are apprehended.

We arrived at our target house and Jerry was all fired up to knock in the door. We are all stacked up and I was number one, so I was the point man and Jerry was number four so he was the door kicker. We were all ready to roll until all of a sudden I saw something and held my hand up to motion, STOP! Then I put my finger next to my mouth and motioned for everyone to shush. There was a broken window in the door. I reached in through the jagged, broken glass and without making a sound I turned the knob. I just opened the door. I could see the look on Jerry's crestfallen face. I had ruined Jerry's moment.

There was no time to dwell on that; we were in the house. We moved from room to room like silent ninjas. When we entered one room I saw that there were people lying on a pallet on the floor on the other side of the room. It was dark except for the lights on the front of our M-4s. I saw in front of me what looked like four people under a blanket. I thought to myself, *There is no way they are still sleeping.* So I looked back at the others and held up two fingers and then pointed them at my eyes. I was telling them to watch the people on the floor. They kept their weapons pointed at these people and I lowered mine. I did have a moment where I thought to myself, *I'm about to either be blown up or shot. Something bad is about to happen here.* I took a deep breath and I leaned over the supposedly sleeping people. I grabbed a corner of the blanket and yanked it back in one jerk. The first thing I noticed was that the woman was completely naked! I froze for a few seconds as I stared at her. I'd been with only men for more than a month, so seeing a naked woman was a shock. I shook off my surprise and we grabbed the parents and two children. The wife threw something around her shoulders and we put the family in another room to question them. We didn't find the teenager we were looking for that day.

We had a couple of really rough days and a few of our guys were killed while we were on a routine mission looking for someone with intel. As I said, this war was a different one from the one I had fought two years earlier. We were fighting to stay alive. And the only way we could do that was if we could find out who was planting the roadside bombs. Where did they store the materials? Who was building them? This was the line of questioning we followed with every person we apprehended.

We would tell them, "If you aren't with the enemy then talk to us. Help us help you." For the most part they did. We were there, after all, to restore order and peace. But there was still an enemy to defeat and our most pressing matter was the bombs. So while we were following up on a tip about a guy believed to be involved, we lost two of our own.

My anger was at a boiling point. No matter how hard I worked to suppress my feelings about Ravago's death, I had my triggers. The anger would resurface and it was nasty.

We stopped a car and the guy seemed suspicious, so we grabbed him for questioning. We had him flex-cuffed and seated on the curb. Jerry and the others were talking to him and I was standing there with them. Only I wasn't really there. Not mentally, anyway. It was like being somewhere in a tunnel where I could only kind of hear what was going on. I was in a haze of anger. My jaw was clenched and my fists were balled up. I heard them say something about not being able to get anything out of this guy—that they were going to just let him go. And just like a flame to a fuse I exploded with one powerful punch. Everyone reacted and started yelling at me. Someone said he was going to tell Sergeant Gebhardt, our platoon sergeant. I knew what I had done was wrong. I knew I had lost my cool and that I had been unprofessional.

At this point my platoon was on our thirty-day duty at the bridge. We were staying in this two-story building adjacent to the bridge. When we got back I ignored everyone and just walked straight up the two flights and then out to the ladder that led to the roof. I climbed the rungs of that ladder and hoisted myself up on the roof, away from the noise. I sat there staring at the Euphrates River. Sergeant Gebhardt quietly came behind me and sat down next to me. After a few minutes he said, "You know it can't be like that, right?"

"I know. I know I shouldn't have done that. I know that taking my anger out on innocent people is not going to achieve anything," I said.

And then I just broke down. In fits and starts between chest-heaving sobs I talked about Ravago. I talked about the guys we lost earlier that week. I talked about how mad I was that other guys had lost their lives.

"I know not everyone in this country is to blame, but it's hard to not have that anger," I moaned.

Gebhardt listened patiently and nodded sympathetically, and then he said, "I know, man. But it just can't happen like that. But this doesn't have to go any further than this."

And that was it. I didn't get in trouble. I knew what I had done was wrong and am thankful that I didn't cause any worse damage. I did not think of myself as a violent man. But the more times we were attacked, the more lives we lost, the harder it was to keep those demons at bay. It was another moment I found myself thankful to have Jerry. He was the rational, intelligent

LIVING WITH NO EXCUSES   101

one. He kept me from letting the anger completely consume me and from doing anything really stupid. He prevented me from running wild through the streets of Yusafiah.

But it was clear I was losing my grip on reality. One evening I was on the roof of a building at an intersection in some little town. I wasn't wearing my helmet or my vest. I was just in a T-shirt. The roofs were flat and there was about a two-foot-high wall at the ledge. I stood there with my right foot propped up on the wall and looked out at the little town. I felt fueled with power. Like I was having the ultimate manly man moment. I could see then why people say power is addictive. I felt high on it in that moment. All my life I had strived to be "manly." Everything I did was about being "the man." And in that moment that is how I felt: completely dominant. As I stood on that roof unprotected and not giving a shit, I looked out over the town and said to myself, but as if I were talking to all of them, "Work with me or against me. I can either destroy you or I can help you." I believed every word of that. Nothing could touch me. No one could hurt me. I was completely invincible.

CHAPTER 10

And Then I Got Blown Up

(December 2005)

MORALE AT the potato warehouse had hit an all-time low and the danger outside of it couldn't have been higher. Things were very bad. My company commander seemed to have given up on life. He wasn't even in his uniform anymore. He wandered around the potato warehouse like a zombie wearing nothing but his PTs—a pair of black army shorts and a T-shirt, untucked. Everyone was in rough shape and nothing was going as it should have gone.

Back in basic training, I'd been assigned to be a mortarman. But I hated that and knew I only wanted infantry. But I was put through the mortar classes and I learned the basics. When the mortarmen go out on a mission there is a guy who is the FO, the forward observer. His job is to observe the situation and call back the coordinates of the target he wants to hit. The mortarmen then put the coordinates in and if the FO wants to change anything he will say, "Adjust fire." Then the mortarmen make the adjustment and fire the mortars toward the target.

One day there was a call for a mortar mission and the FO didn't want to leave the safety of the potato plant. It wasn't that safe in there but I guess he thought it was better than leaving. So even though he was an officer, he sent out a guy lower in rank and experience. The guy he sent was giving out bad coordinates. There was a lot of commotion and shouting and contradiction.

"I don't know where anything is. I don't see it."

"We're putting the coordinates where you told us to put them."

All of a sudden one of the guys rushed into the potato warehouse screaming. Our mortars had struck a farm. A family was working out in their field right where we hit. They'd been blown up. One of the men in my platoon rushed in the injured mother and two little boys, a six-year-old and an eight-year-old. The medics got to work right away and my buddy Ryan and I stepped up to help. Ryan knew a little Arabic, so he could talk to the kids. He introduced himself to the six-year-old lying on a stretcher, his body riddled with shrapnel. And as if he didn't feel a thing, the little boy looked up at Ryan, stuck his hand out, and introduced himself. He was so calm and brave. Ryan stayed with him and I stayed with his brother until we loaded them up on the helicopter and sent them to a camp where they could be treated properly. The six-year-old didn't make it. Ryan never really recovered emotionally from that.

After that it became clear that if we were going to treat women and children, we would need a female medic to join our medical unit. Ashley Voss was a medic stationed with the battalion and she heard about this. By now everyone knew that where we were was incredibly dangerous. It was dangerous where the battalion was stationed as well, but we had it far worse at the potato plant. In spite of the danger, Ashley marched right up to the battalion commander and said, "You need to send me to Bravo Company. They need a female medic. I need to be there. I can help."

The colonel said, "You're crazy. I am not going to send you there. It's too dangerous."

But Ashley is the kind of person who, if she wants to do something, will make it happen. Finally she got the battalion commander to agree. She was coming to Bravo Company. At this point we had completed our rotation at the bridge and intersection jobs and we were back at the potato plant pulling security. We were also the quick reaction force should anybody need it. And we were available if anyone needed a run to battalion for supplies or anything else, so we got the call to pick up the female medic.

We loaded up in the Humvees and headed out right before dark. I was in the driver's seat and I knew we were coming to where the road hits a T intersection. But I just flew down this road—feeling absolutely no fear, thinking about the female medic we were about to add to our unit. One of the guys from headquarters platoon was riding with me and my driving completely stressed him out. I got a kick out of that. As we got closer to the intersection he got more and more anxious. "Noah, you may want to slow down. You gotta make this turn," he sputtered. I waved him off. "I got it." And he said, with a little more urgency, "You gotta make this turn!" I didn't slow down. I yanked the wheel and skidded us around to the right, never letting my foot off the gas. It's not like these Humvees can travel at a high rate of speed. We could get them up to sixty, seventy miles per hour at best. But they're pretty heavy and when I made that turn and the weight shifted left, I thought the vehicle was going to go up on two wheels. The frantic screams of my passenger would have made flipping the Humvee completely worth it.

We arrived at battalion just as it was getting dark. Ryan's wife was a mechanic at battalion and he'd asked me to go see her. She had a carton of cigarettes to give him. I asked if he needed anything else before I left and he said, "Nah. Tell her I love her." I told him I would. So when I got there I went straight to see her. She led me into this little café and we sat down with some hot tea. She gave me the cigarettes and we talked for a while about this and that and as I stood up to head out she said, "Hey, Noah, be careful out there. It's dangerous where y'all are at." I tilted my head to the side and said, "Be careful? I'm Noah, what can happen to me?" I smiled cockily and walked out.

I got back to the vehicles and spotted Ashley Voss right away. She was standing there waiting with her rucksack, ready to go. I walked up to her, smiled, and said, "Hey, what's up? I'm Noah."

"Hi. I'm Ashley," she said without much emotion.

"Cool. Are you excited to come to our area?" I flashed her a grin.

After a brief pause she said, "Yeah, the medics can use a female."

She was acting like a professional and I was acting more like someone standing at a bar trying to buy her a drink. As if that couldn't be more awkward, right at that moment my radio squawked loudly, "Hey, can somebody get me that female medic's roster number? I need it before we head out." It was Jerry, ruining my game.

I leaned over and hit the button and said a little too proudly, "I've got the female medic with me now. I will get that for you."

And before I could ask her what it was, Jerry came back over the radio, "Galloway. You're with the female. Why am I not surprised?" Ashley gave me her roster number, and I sent it back to Jerry.

I turned to Ashley and said, "I'm not a player, just wanted to know more about you."

She didn't look that convinced. We got in the trucks and drove back. At the potato plant all the guys started sniffing this girl out like a bunch of hound dogs. One of the guys ran and grabbed her rucksack for her and carried it into the medic station, like he was a bellhop.

Each of the line platoons—first, second, and third—had its own assigned medic. Harley Shanklin was second platoon's medic. Then there was a head medic for the company with head-quarters platoon, and then there was Captain Segui. He was a physician's assistant. This medical team was responsible for the whole company, about a hundred and fifty people. Now that Ashley was there she would assist that team whenever they needed it and she would step up in particular if wounded women and children were in our care.

The next day Captain Goodwin pulled Jerry aside and showed him a map on the wall that covered our entire area—an image from a specialized camera—and said that he saw something he thought was hidden weapons.

"Yeah, we need to go out and find something here," said Captain Goodwin as he spread both his arms over the map. Jerry looked annoyed and asked, "Can you be more specific?"

"There has to be something we can find, a weapons cache or something. Go patrol this area," Captain Goodwin said, again while pointing to a map of our whole area.

Jerry shrugged and muttered, "Whatever." He motioned for us all to head out on what he felt was a useless patrol—a wild-goose chase. But we only had half of our platoon on this day. Colonel Punk issued an order asking half of our platoon to help bring in more gravel to the small camp where battalion was housed. They needed gravel because the camp was currently all sand and dirt, which turned to mud if it rained. In order to bring in gravel, dump trucks had to be used. And to get dump trucks there full of gravel, they needed a group of infantry soldiers to pull security and drive the trucks in with a full convoy of Humvees. Here we were, a company that was maxed out, in an area that was too big for us, with people sitting out in intersections everywhere. We just didn't have enough manpower for everything. First platoon was getting hit. They'd lost a lot of guys. They were almost to the point where first platoon was in danger of being shut down because they'd been hit so hard and had so few men left. And now we were being forced to send half of second platoon to pull security for a camp we didn't even live on. Another stupid decision by a poor leader.

But an order is an order, so we split in two. Half of our platoon went on the gravel mission. The other half went on Captain Goodwin's magical mystery tour for a weapons cache hidden somewhere in Yusafiah. As we drove around, Captain Goodwin was back at the potato warehouse calling in to Jerry every five minutes giving him different directions as to where this mysterious place might be. He was watching infrared drone cameras.

Jerry was convinced he was just looking at different mounds of dirt. We drove around, got out, walked around, got back in the car, and drove around some more.

Then we saw a little white pickup truck. As soon as the driver saw us, he took off. That was suspicious, so we headed after the guy. He turned and crossed a bridge over a canal and then turned past some trees. For once I was not driving our vehicle. But the guy who was driving stopped abruptly. Through the front windshield we stared at this rinky-dink little bridge. We all shouted at him to cross it, but he wouldn't budge.

"That bridge can't handle us!" he yelled. We all yelled back at him to go. The only reason I wasn't driving that day was that Sergeant Gebhardt, our platoon sergeant, told me he didn't want me driving the vehicles. The drivers were often hit by roadside bombs. He also didn't want Jerry and me riding in the same Humvee. He couldn't afford to lose us both at the same time. He saw us as two critical members of the platoon. There was also a close bond among Gebhardt, Jerry, and me. But that second rule was a lot harder to keep. Jerry and I would sometimes go off by ourselves to check something out we thought was suspicious. It was mostly because I talked Jerry into that kind of crazy renegade stuff. Most of the time Jerry was too smart to do stupid things like that, but every once in a while I could persuade him. That day, however, I followed one of the rules. I wasn't driving.

When our driver that day made a fuss about the bridge I got mad and told Jerry, "See, this is why I need to be driving. We could be driving down a road with a cliff to the right and if you said turn right, I'll turn right. We don't need people driving who are gonna panic and not do what they gotta do," I said.

Jerry hushed me. We'd lost the little white truck anyway so we returned to our original mission. We kept driving until we came to an empty canal that was very deep. We got out and Jerry said, "I guess we'll just have to cross this on foot and go over there to find whatever Captain Goodwin thinks he sees."

"I can get the Humvee through that," I said.

Jerry looked over and down and said, "No, there's no way."

"Y'all go ahead and walk, I'll worry about the Humvee," I said. So they all got out of the vehicle and began to cross through the canal on foot. I assessed the situation and then backed up the vehicle. I threw it into drive and gunned the gas. The engine was so loud that the sound bounced off the trees. *RAAARRR.* I drove that truck right down the first side of the canal and came barreling up the other side. The nine-thousand-pound vehicle flew out of that canal. Once I roared through the canal, the Humvee behind me followed suit. We pulled up next to Jerry and five other members of our squad like a taxi service. Jerry was so stunned he didn't even yell at me for acting like a fool. What was he going to say? "Don't do that again"?

"Okay, I guess we can walk or we can drive," Jerry said. They all got back in and we drove a little farther before stopping to get out and once again look for Captain Goodwin's secret bunker. We were all griping that there was nothing there and the sun was starting to set. We kept walking anyway into an area where we were surrounded by canals. The canals had big, thick reeds, almost like trees, growing up from them so it was hard to see what was inside the reeds or to the other side of the canals. And then all of a sudden, as we were walking we saw something run through the weeds in one of the canals. It was large and black, a blur it was moving so fast. Now we were all chattering at once. *What was that?*

"That was a cougar. It had to be a cougar," I said.

"No, that was a bear. Looked like a bear to me. That was a bear," Jerry said.

"You know when we invaded a lot of animals escaped from the zoo. It could have been a cougar."

Jerry again said it was a bear and then one of the other guys said, "There are no bears in this part of the world."

This silly argument went on for quite a while. We were all laughing and having a good time. Our mission had been pointless, so this helped lighten the mood. Someone even said they thought it was a ninja because a ninja is just as plausible as a bear or a cougar in the middle of Iraq.

After our good laugh at the mysterious exotic animal running wild through the canals, Jerry called it a day. We weren't finding anything and it was getting dark. As we headed out, one of our vehicles got stuck in some mud in an open field. It took us a while to get it out, and by the time we did the sun had set. We were forced to use our headlights. We knew we'd run the risk of drawing attention to ourselves so we headed back to the potato plant as soon as we could. When we got in I was beat and went to lie down. If you weren't pulling security or assigned to another job, it was best to try to catch some shut-eye while you could.

I had just drifted off to sleep when Jerry woke me up. "Hey, we're going to take the Humvees and pick up the rest of the platoon. They're done with the gravel run. There's no mission. We need empty seats in the Humvee. I just wanted you to know that we're leaving. Go back to sleep," Jerry whispered.

I leapt right off my cot and said, "No, sir. If you go, I go. If y'all go and something happens I will never forgive myself. And what if y'all get into an awesome firefight? I'm itching for that. I'm not going to miss that. I am going and I am driving the lead vehicle."

Jerry protested. "What about Gebhardt? He doesn't want you driving."

"He can yell at me when we get there," I said.

"It doesn't matter. Let's just go. And I want to drive. I never get to drive," Jerry said.

"Jerry, you're not driving. You can ride in the Humvee with me but you're not driving. I'm not going to let you."

Now, Jerry outranked me, which meant he could do whatever he wanted. But that was also why he wasn't supposed to drive. I was talking to Jerry as a friend now, though. I reminded him of that conversation we had in the gym before we deployed.

"I told you that I was never going to let anything happen to you. I would jump in front of a bullet to keep you from getting hurt. Nothing will ever happen to you while I'm around. You're not driving." He finally relented and said, "Okay."

We piled into the Humvees and headed out. Jerry rode with me in the lead vehicle. That's not following protocol. The platoon leader should be in the middle of the convoy, but neither Jerry nor I ever wanted to be there. We wanted to be in the lead, always.

Standard procedure for nighttime driving was to drive with no headlights. You don't want to announce to the enemy where you are. We all wore night-vision goggles so we could see. It was only about ten miles to the battalion's outpost camp. We'd driven this road a million times before. No one was tense or worried about anything. It was the main road between our base and battalion base, and it was generally clear.

On the way, there was an Iraqi checkpoint. The Iraqi Army set up there to check civilians as they came through. These checkpoints were designed to slow people down, and were made up of concrete barriers constructed in a zigzag pattern. As U.S. military we were not required to stop. But this particular checkpoint was on a road with canals on either side. We couldn't fly by it or drive around it like some of the other checkpoints. My only choice was to drive through it. I knew that the best way to beat a roadside bomb is to speed through the part of the road where it might be lurking. At the time, the type of explosives the enemy placed in the roadways had the smallest delay from trigger to explosion. So the faster we drove, the less likely we were to feel the brunt of the blast. That's why I never slowed down to take a turn. But in this case, I had no choice. I had to slow down to get through the zigzags.

After making my way through and pulling out of the last barrier I took off. I started to pick up speed just as we turned around a curve in the road. The road was alongside a canal, but there was about twenty feet of gravel between the two.

Jerry was seated next to me in shotgun. He later said that for a brief second he saw out of the corner of his eye a bush that didn't quite look right on the side of the road. But it was too late. Just as he saw it and before he could turn back to me to say anything, I'd driven the front tires right over a trip wire. There was a bright flash of light. That's one of the problems with wearing night-vision goggles. You can see most things, but you can't see a trip wire. The trip wire led straight into that bush and detonated a bomb hidden inside it powerful enough to slam my driver's-side door so hard it threw our nine-thousand-pound Humvee clear off the road. We went flying into the air and tumbled down into a deep canal. We rolled over and then landed, thankfully wheels down, in the water. I was knocked out cold. Jerry was stunned but alert. Our gunner, Ryan Davis, was stunned; his leg was hurt, but otherwise he was okay.

Jerry came to and realized he couldn't see anything. His night-vision goggles had been folded down over his helmet and were shattered. His helmet was cracked, so he took it off. When he looked down he saw water swirling under his feet.

Jerry shouted, "Is everyone all right?" Ryan answered but I didn't. I was out cold. Jerry said he called my name a few more times but there was no response. Jerry pushed his way to the back and out of the top of the truck. He climbed down into the canal and waded through waist-deep water toward the driver's-side door. The Humvee was tilted away from him and the road, which kept me higher up in the water. He couldn't see much, so he turned his flashlight on and raised it up and into the driver's-side window. The funnel of light from his flashlight gave Jerry his first glimpse of just how badly hurt I was. My arm and leg were mangled and he wasn't sure if I was dead or alive. He said he saw my vest move up and down and thought, *Okay, he's alive. For now.*

Jerry scrambled up the canal to the side of the road to check on the two other vehicles we had had with us. It turns out that when the bomb detonated, the explosion was so bright it blinded the other men in the other trucks momentarily. They did what we always did when we encountered roadside bombs: they kept driving. They assumed we did, too. They thought we were way ahead of them.

Jerry started to worry that we were about to be ambushed. He didn't have a helmet anymore to protect himself. He saw there was one on the side of the road and grabbed it quickly to put it on. It was mangled and when he tipped it over, blood poured out. My name was on the helmet. Jerry climbed back down into the canal to check on me again. I was still completely unconscious. My arm was hanging on by ligaments. Jerry is a very religious man and he just stood in that cold water looking at me and prayed.

Just then the other two Humvees in our convoy came tearing back down the road toward us. They'd realized there was no way we would be that far ahead of them, so they'd come back to the site of the explosion. Jerry's wrist was broken and his face was all cut up from the bulletproof glass in the shattered windshield. Jerry looked up and saw that help was coming. He climbed up to the road to flag them down and the other guys saw him and Ryan and asked, "Where's Noah?" He pointed down to the canal.

Jerry shook off his shock and went back to platoon leader mode. He started issuing orders. "All right, set security. Get a couple of guys down there. We gotta get Galloway outta there."

They struggled to get me out. My legs were a mangled mess of flesh and metal under the water. As they were trying to pull me out, Jerry got on the radio and called back to the company. "We've been hit. Galloway is either hurt or dead. Our gunner is hurt. We need some people out here now. We barely have enough people for security and we're trying to get Noah out of the canal."

The company commander, Captain Goodwin, replied over the radio, "We don't have anybody. There is nobody we can send. Y'all gotta get out of there."

He was right. We didn't have enough people. Our company was as thinned out as it could be.

But another convoy heard this traffic on the radio. They piped in and said, "We're near there. We're coming." A little while later a convoy of three more Humvees pulled up to help. They were able to assist our guys and get me out of the truck and up that steep embankment. They threw me into one of their Humvees and rushed me back to the potato plant.

Back at the plant the medics were ready. They knew I was coming and they knew it was bad. Captain Segui gathered the team and said, "When he comes in here, you get one stick to hit a vein. If you don't get him in the first stick, we're hitting him in the chest. We've got to get fluid in him." Captain Segui said that he thought I'd gone so long without blood to my brain, I'd never walk or talk again, but he had to try to save my life.

After we had first set up in the potato plant and I met Captain Segui, I had made it a point to be overly enthusiastic whenever I saw him. "Hey, sir, how are you doing today? Good morning, sir. Do you need anything, sir?" And he would laugh and say, "No, Galloway, I'm good." People would ask, "Galloway, why are you so happy to see Captain Segui?" I'd say, "I want him to like me. If something ever happens to me, I want him to work really hard."

I knew he worked hard on all of his patients, but I think my campaign worked. He was on that night. He was not going to let me die. I needed blood, but they didn't have any. They did have some chemical that confuses the body into thinking it is blood, so they pumped me full of that. At that point, I woke up a little bit. I wasn't lucid but apparently I was conscious and contentious. I was fighting and grunting. They tried to give me oxygen, but I wouldn't let them stick a tube down my throat or even put a mask over my face. I was fighting everyone. They had to hold me down.

Captain Segui then asked Ashley to sit by my ear and talk to me. She said she didn't know what to say, but started talking anyway. She said whatever came to her mind. She talked about how she'd once visited Alabama while part of a bachelorette party. I don't remember anything about this night except for that. I remembered what she said to me. And it worked. I calmed down. They'd been able to put tourniquets on to slow the bleeding of my wounds. She calmed me down enough for them to work and eventually I passed out. I don't think anyone there that night had much faith I'd ever wake up again. This was when Jerry came in to check on me. He asked how I was and Captain Segui shook his head and said, "We lost another one."

Jerry needed attention for his wounds as well, so they put both of us onto a helicopter to take us to the hospital in Baghdad. I was on a gurney and Jerry was seated in front of me, carefully resting his bandaged wrist on his lap, just looking at me. He was teary and praying and then all of a sudden I abruptly sat straight up and was just looking around and apparently yelling like a zombie. He said it was like a drunk person who'd suddenly woken up somewhere he didn't recognize. The crew chief on the helicopter pushed me back down. He held me down like that until we landed in Baghdad. I have no memory of this whatsoever but we were taken into the CASH—Combat Army Surgical Hospital— and Jerry and I were separated.

CHAPTER 11

Sweet Home Alabama

(September 2006–March 2007)

I WAS SO HAPPY to be home and settling into my new house, where I could be with Colston all the time, as well as Tracy. There was no sort of residual feeling about Brandi, nor was there any guilt. It was obvious to me that in the beginning Brandi and I had been great together, but after a while we just didn't fit right. And we were so young. We were still teenagers when we got married. But with Tracy, it was different. I truly felt she could be the one. I asked Tracy to move in with me.

I come from a family where you don't just ask a girl to move in with you. That's not very proper. But regardless, my mom was so excited I was moving back home that she wanted to throw me a housewarming party. Mostly the party was full of my mom's friends and it became pretty clear that she had not told any of them that Tracy was living with me. The ladies were all abuzz with compliments about the house, saying things like, "Oh, didn't Noah do really good decorating his house?"

Tracy had to bite her lip not to say, "Well, actually, I did all of this." But she didn't say it. She pulled me aside and said, "I'm pretty sure none of these people knows that I live here." I looked at her and smiled and said, "That's possible. Just go with it." She laughed and we kept it at that.

Those first several months I was happy. Being with Tracy and Colston distracted me from all of the unresolved issues I felt about Iraq, about my injuries, and about my uncertain future. She also helped me cope with the little moments when I forgot to be distracted. She cut up my steak for me when we went out. One time when I couldn't open a jar I got very mad. But she just came over and opened it for me. She didn't make a big deal about it; she just did it. I told her, "You know how hard that is as a man to have you open a jar for me? I am supposed to be doing these things for you and I can't." But she told me that was no big deal. And she made me feel like it wasn't.

I struggled a little with Colston as well. I was capable of taking care of him in many ways, but it was hard and little things would trip me up. Putting a sock on a toddler with one hand will absolutely stress you out. It's funny now, looking back. But back then I really struggled to get a sock on that boy.

When Colston wasn't there we went out with friends a lot. We even turned my garage into a little bar with a pool table and would have our friends over all the time. I got along with her family and she got along with mine. She was great with Colston, too. I knew I wanted to marry her. We even talked about it but I told her not to expect it this year. Then I went out and bought a ring.

I went to Tracy's dad to get his permission and he was fine with it. Then I went to Tracy's stepdad and he was happy about it. Everyone knew it was coming but no one knew when. Including myself. I was waiting for the right moment to present itself. Right before Christmas we were going to take a trip to Nashville to visit Tim Humbert, a buddy I served with on my first deployment in 2003. He and his wife had invited us to visit.

I had the ring with me on this trip. I was still looking for the perfect moment to ask her, so I wanted to make sure I had it with me all the time. I wanted her to have that fairy-tale proposal moment. In the very back of my Jeep there was a five-disk CD changer that didn't work, so the casing was out. I hid the ring back there. When we arrived in Nashville the Humberts suggested we should all go see the Rockettes. They were performing at the Opry Mills mall. We all agreed and Tim said he wanted to drive.

I almost always would prefer that I drive instead of someone else but I didn't think anything of it and agreed to ride with them. So we got there and saw there was an ice exhibit set up with all of these amazing ice carvings. We walked through it before the show. I started looking around and realized that this was a magical winter wonderland. What an amazing place to propose to Tracy! And then I remembered I didn't have the ring! There was even a room that didn't have a ton of people milling around, and was filled with ice sculptures and this pretty soft light in little spotlights from the ceiling. What a wasted opportunity!

The next day Tracy said she wanted to go shopping. Back we went to Opry Mills. We shopped and were enjoying ourselves and having just a really nice day together. Tracy bought a new pair of shoes because her feet were killing her. She didn't want to carry around her old shoes all day so we walked back to the car for her to change them. I looked around and realized it was just the two of us in the parking lot. I opened the back of the Jeep so she had a place to sit and change her shoes. I thought there probably was no better time or place than right there. She loves the mall. Why not? I reached past her, grabbed the ring, and asked her to marry me in the Opry Mills parking lot.

We set the date for St. Patrick's Day 2006. It was exactly one year from Tracy and Seth's trip to visit me at Walter Reed. There was also a lot of family significance. My grandmother on my dad's side of the family is a Flynn, so, of course, her family is Irish. Tracy's last name is Ennis, and her family has Irish roots, too, so it seemed like March 17 was a perfect day to get hitched. In the process of planning the wedding, Tracy decided she wanted to start going to church more. I agreed. We picked the church her granddaddy went to and where my sisters went as well.

So it was a family affair at this itty-bitty Baptist church. Tracy started to get more involved with the church and then she started meeting with the preacher regularly. She wanted me to come with her, so I did. Right away there was something about this guy I didn't trust. It had nothing to do with his faith. I just felt there was something off about him. They start talking about Tracy being born again and they ask me if I wanted to be as well. I was uncomfortable with this and said, "You know what, now is not the time. I should probably feel it and I'm not feeling it. So I'm good."

The preacher didn't care for that. He started threatening to not let us get married at his church. But thankfully, because Tracy's granddaddy went there and my sisters went there, he relented and agreed we could go ahead with our wedding as planned in the church, which made Tracy so happy. Her granddaddy was also ordained, so we were able to have him officiate instead of the disgruntled preacher.

The wedding festivities were a lot of fun. A bunch of my buddies came to town and stayed with me the night before, and Tracy went to her friend's house. My guys and I woke up in the morning, drank a couple of shots, and were like, "All right! Let's go to a wedding!" We got to the church, took a few "before" pictures, and then it was showtime.

I was standing in front of the congregation next to Tracy's granddad waiting for the service to start. The church was busting at the seams with guests. I was very excited to marry Tracy. After a few minutes I said under my breath and through clenched teeth, "Man, what is taking so long?" I turned and looked at everyone out in the pews and shouted, "She's coming! I promise!" and everyone laughed. I thought a little humor would lighten the mood. Finally someone opened the door and gave me a thumbs-up.

Then the procession started. All of the groomsmen and bridesmaids happily marched down the aisle, and then the music changed and all heads turned toward the back of the room. Tracy walked through the door looking absolutely beautiful. A giant smile spread across my face and it grew and grew as she walked, arm in arm with her dad, toward me. I was so happy. For her granddad, this was an extra-big day. Tracy was his oldest grandchild and the very first to get married. He was happy, excited, and nervous. In fact, his nerves got the best of him and he rushed through the ceremony. Tracy and I didn't really notice so it didn't affect us at all. But as we get to the reception my buddy Judd came up to me and said, "When the wedding began I just happened to glance at my watch and then y'all were done and it hadn't even been three minutes. And now everyone's drunk, dancing, and partying. That's how you have a wedding."

CHAPTER 12

Finding a
New Normal

(2007–2009)

SHORTLY AFTER I came home to Alabama, Uncle Johnny told me that I needed to enroll right away with the Department of Veterans Affairs. I followed his instructions and went through the process. When I met my doctor for the first time, he explained how their prosthetics coverage works.

"We at the VA have a contract with a couple of the prosthetic companies, but you can go see whomever you want. Even if they are not part of the VA program, wherever you decide to do prosthetics, we cover that," he said.

He told me this with representatives in the room from four of the prosthetic companies in different regions of Alabama. I recognized one of the reps. On one of my visits home from Walter Reed I had forgotten my charger for my leg. This fellow named

Dan at Birmingham Limb and Brace helped me out. I didn't have any other evidence or criteria to judge by, so I said I'd go with them. They were excited to be treating someone they saw as a strong, athletic amputee. Right away they suggested that I get a running leg. I thought that sounded like a great idea.

Within a couple of months, I heard about the Lakeshore Foundation in Homewood, Alabama, and went to check it out. I wasn't sure what to expect. I'd just been told they work with a lot of amputees. While I was there I learned that Lakeshore is one of seven Olympic and Paralympic training sites in the United States. They focus specifically on Paralympic athletes. The U.S. wheelchair basketball team trains there. It's not just for those elite athletes, though. It's a full-service sports facility for disabled athletes and sports enthusiasts alike. It has everything you could ever want if you have a disability but still want to exercise or train.

They told me that they were starting a program for injured veterans and that they would love for me to be involved. A lot of people wanted to help wounded veterans. Most had really great intentions and many were veterans themselves. So a lot of different organizations sprang up at this time with the purpose of helping injured veterans rehabilitate and adjust to life post-injury.

The Lakeshore Foundation realized that there was an entire new group of people in need of their services. The people at Lakeshore came at this issue from a unique perspective. I loved their concepts and their approach. They worked with people with disabilities every day and always had. They were also all very athletic and pushed themselves every day. Veterans were treated no differently from their other clients. The people at Lakeshore had no problem saying, "You can do this. Let us show you someone who is worse off than you who has already done it." I loved that approach. They took my excuses away. I happily agreed to start working with them on the development of these programs.

I met a lot of really great people through Lakeshore. People like Natalie Hausman-Weiss. She worked in the office at Lakeshore and her son was disabled and wore leg braces. One day she told me, "You should meet Eric Eisenberg. He owns BioTech Limb and Brace and he's about to start doing a running clinic here at Lakeshore Foundation."

"A running clinic sounds really cool, but I'm working with another prosthetics company. Is that okay?" I responded.

Natalie assured me that it was okay. All prosthetic companies were invited and it was open to everyone. Eric really just wanted to work with athletic people who wore braces or prosthetics. She said that I should definitely go. So I thought, *Why not?*

I showed up to the next clinic and met Eric and a few other amputees who were also participating. A Paralympic coach volunteered to run the clinic with Eric. The coach told me that he was very impressed with my strong form. I told him I was just learning. I hadn't had my running leg all that long, after all. He told me that once I got used to the new leg, I would be great. I thought that was a pretty cool compliment coming from a guy who coaches Olympians.

I was also impressed with Eric. Right away there was a genuine connection. As I continued to attend his clinic and got to know him better I decided I should switch to Eric's company. It was hard because I didn't have any issue with Dan or his team at Birmingham Limb and Brace. It was just that I had built a strong friendship with Eric and it felt strange not to go to him for my needs. I was so torn about this issue that I even went to my doctor at the VA before I made the change. The doctor told me, "People switch prosthetic companies all the time. It's not going to bother Birmingham Limb and Brace at all. In fact, when you first came in there were different companies lined up in here. They all get along. They all know each other. It's fine."

He even went so far as to say he'd call them for me and ask them to send over the prosthetics they still had in their office. I thanked him but said no, this was something I needed to handle myself. The next day I went to see Dan. He greeted me warmly and took me back to his office. I said, "Dan, y'all are amazing. The whole staff. I love all of y'all but I kinda want to try other prosthetic companies out and I want to give BioTech a shot."

Dan was touched by my gesture and said, "Noah, I understand. You shouldn't just go to the first prosthetics company you find and stay there. You may like it or you may not. You can always come back to us. I'm really impressed that you came all the way down here just to tell me that. That says a lot about your character."

Eric and I built on a close bond that formed almost immediately. He's been one of my biggest supporters ever since, in good times and bad. When after a while I stopped going to running clinics and stopped running, Eric gently tried to motivate me. He didn't push me or shame me but he let me know he was there to help me find my way when I was ready.

He sat me down one day and said, "If you want to get back in shape, I will pay for your gym membership. I'll pay for a personal trainer. You just let me know. Noah, there are hundreds of other injured veterans out there, but they don't all have what you have. You have a natural athletic ability and a level of fitness most others don't and never will. This is how you will stand out from the rest now. Just let me know when you're ready."

I still had a lot of ups and downs to go through before I really understood what Eric meant that day, but I knew I had somebody I could count on.

CHAPTER 13

Slowly Filling with Darkness

(2007–2009)

TRACY AND I had what I thought was a really good start. We were in love, had a wonderful wedding, and were having fun as a married couple. We enjoyed going out drinking with our friends, as many do in their twenties. But other than that, we weren't really developing the foundations of a solid marriage. My mom was the first to point it out. "Y'all are never together," she'd say a lot. And, honestly, I didn't think this was a bad thing.

On the weekends when I had Colston, it was just Daddy-and-Colston time. Tracy would happily go out with her girlfriends. When I didn't have Colston, Tracy worked during the week, so on weeknights I went out drinking with my friends. Nothing seemed wrong about this to me. For a large part of our courtship, Tracy and I lived in different time zones and saw each other only on the weekends. This seemed to be the perfect arrangement as far as I was concerned. We wouldn't get irritated or sick of each other. I felt that, in the end, Tracy and I were smothering each other. But Mom was right. I just didn't realize it. We weren't forming a bond as a couple.

I also wasn't opening up to her, even though emotional things were really beginning to stir under the surface for me. I didn't realize that anything was going on with me, of course. But I would stay up late at night and drink by myself a lot. I would just stare at videos online. It quickly became obvious that I was an angry person. I would get irritated and upset all the time. But never about anything you'd guess would make someone that mad. Tracy used to say, "You know, the big things you don't worry about. But something little happens and you lose your mind." And she was right. If money was tight and she was stressed about paying bills, I'd be calm and collected and say, "It's okay." But say I went through a drive-through to get something to take home and they forgot to put in the packet of sour cream or to put pickles on my sandwich. I would absolutely lose it. I would pitch a fit or break something.

So, yeah, we weren't spending that much time together. Honestly, she just didn't want to be around me, and who could blame her? I was an angry person.

I didn't understand it yet. I had no idea why I was feeling the way I did. I was completely clueless. Fairly often I would come across someone who would say to me, "It must be hard to be missing two limbs." And I would reply, "Nah, it ain't that hard."

I was bottling everything up. I was portraying myself as a superhero nobody could touch. I think on some level I still thought I could be that carefree little boy with the towel cape, that somehow I could get away with still wearing that disguise. In reality I was pushing everything I felt back and deep down inside. I was bottling it all up and I was sinking into a deep depression, because I was wearing a mask. I couldn't let anyone down. I couldn't show anyone any weakness. I was falling deeper and deeper into this dark place because I couldn't open up to anyone.

One day I was out running errands and had my first panic attack. I'd never had one before so it was exceptionally terrifying to feel this sudden shortness of breath. I was headed to Wal-Mart but didn't make it there. When the attack hit, I just turned the car around and came straight home. I walked in the house and I just lost it. I was crying uncontrollably and had no explanation as to why. Tracy sat with me, but I think it caught her off guard. Other than that one day in the hospital back when she first came to see me, I'd never acted like that. I hadn't cried in front of her. She didn't know how to react. She eventually calmed me down and we carried on with our day as if nothing had happened. That was the only way I could handle it—pretend it didn't happen because I was so embarrassed to have broken down in front of her. In hindsight that probably wasn't a good sign. If you can't break down in front of your spouse then when can you? But I didn't have anybody I felt safe enough with to do that. I saw crying and breaking down as an embarrassment and left it alone.

Tracy and I were still able to carry on and have good moments, though. One of them led to her getting pregnant with Jack. I was so happy to be having another child. But I was completely terrified because I knew emotionally I was a complete wreck and was afraid I wouldn't be capable of being a good father.

When Jack was born in November 2007, I loved him and I was so glad he was here, but I felt helpless. When Colston was born I changed diapers. I was able to help out a lot. But with Jack I felt I couldn't do anything at all for him. I spent time with him but I couldn't change his diaper. Well, if no one else was around to help, I could get through a diaper change, but there would be shit everywhere. A squirming, naked baby is a lot to handle with one hand. But he was so adorable and such a happy baby. Tracy's family lived close by so they were a big help. Jack was the first grandchild on her side, so he got plenty of attention from those grandparents.

After Jack's birth Tracy fell into postpartum depression. This deepened the rift between us and fed into my own depression. I couldn't see it at the time, but we were toxic for each other.

Two years later, in October 2009, Rian was born. I am so glad we didn't stop with Jack because after two boys I was really hoping for a little girl. And there she was. Beautiful and perfect. I was just like every other father—instantly wrapped around the finger of my precious baby girl. But she made me work for her love. I was constantly giving her attention and wanting to hold her and all she wanted was Tracy. It would drive me crazy. I always joke that she came out of the womb a grown woman. She knew how to make me work for her attention.

On the surface we had a perfect family. But if you looked closer, we were unraveling. Even with my delight in having another child, I again was no help. I still couldn't change diapers. I still wasn't much help with the other day-to-day chores of caring for children. I could love them but I physically wasn't capable of small tasks.

As I was falling victim to my depression, Tracy too was struggling. The postpartum depression she'd suffered after Jack was born had never fully gone away. My behavior certainly hadn't helped. Tracy felt alone. And we drifted further apart. We started sleeping in separate rooms. I'd take Jack in the bedroom early in the evening and we'd go to sleep. Tracy would keep Rian with her and stay up late on the couch watching movies. And when the kids weren't around, I was drinking a lot. This wasn't the way to raise a family.

I started to realize that I needed to be better. I needed to be a better father and I needed to change. But my life is no Hollywood story. There was no single "ah-hah" moment. I had several events that eventually got me going in the right direction but it took several attempts. And several pitfalls.

It started with, much like Michael Jackson sang, the man in the mirror. We had a full-length mirror in our bedroom and I would stand in front of it and stare at myself. I couldn't stand what I saw. I'd look at my injuries and I was just disgusted. And then one day I was looking in the mirror and I saw how out of shape I was. It was the worst shape I'd ever been in. And then it was almost as if a switch was flipped in my brain.

I suddenly realized I needed to quit concentrating on what I'd lost. Instead I needed to concentrate on what I had left. I had three beautiful children. I was looking in the mirror at a man who wasn't living up to the promises I had made to each of them. I wasn't being a good father. And then the most terrifying thought crossed my mind. I was showing Jack and Colston what it means to be a man, and they would grow up to be that man. And I was showing Rian how a man is supposed to act. That would be the kind of man she would look for. And it scared me and rocked me to my core. I didn't have a lot of time. They were growing up and I was showing this image of a disgruntled, angry person to my children. I wasn't being much of a man. I had to change.

I flirted with getting back into shape a few times. Eric Eisenberg had told me back when I first met him that he would support me whenever and however I needed it. He'd offered to pay for a gym membership and a trainer. So I finally accepted his help. He set me up with a personal trainer and I worked out with him for about two months. But then I just quit. Eric was supportive but I just wasn't emotionally there yet. I gave up and went back to drinking.

CHAPTER 14

Ten Days in the County Jail

ONE THING about my depression: I hid it very well. Now, looking back, it was pretty obvious. So I guess the more accurate statement is that the person I was hiding from the most was myself. I would go out drinking all the time. But in my mind, I was just going out with friends. I've always been a pretty sociable guy, so I had several groups of friends. I would go out with different ones on different nights. I had a drinking-with-friends schedule for pretty much every day of the week. I convinced myself that this was just being social and having fun. The really sad days were the ones where I sat alone in the house and drank. Well, all of it was sad, but I was able to rationalize at least part of it to myself.

I am not proud to admit this, and it's not an excuse, but I can honestly say I feel like I was not myself during this period of time. But I will own up to my faults and admit that while I was drinking all the time, I was also driving myself home afterward in the wee hours of the morning. If and when I was pulled over, because it did happen, the police officers always looked like mine was the car they didn't want to catch. Right away they saw the Purple Heart tag, and then as they reached the car window and saw I was missing an arm and a leg, I could see the dread in their eyes. They didn't want to have to give a ticket or arrest a wounded veteran. I put them in a very awkward position. I often got, "How far do you have to go to get home?" I never went far from home, so most of the time my answer was "I'm pretty close." Then the officer would usually say, "Go straight home." They had to do their jobs, but at the same time, these guys sympathized with me. I felt they probably looked at me and thought, *I don't know how I would react to losing two limbs. I would probably do more than just drink.*

One chilly night I chose to forgo my usual shorts and T-shirt for long pants, so my injuries weren't as glaringly obvious as they normally were. An officer was patrolling that area because of reports of drag racing and I just happened to be driving a souped-up Camaro. As soon as he approached me he could tell I'd been drinking. He asked me to step out of the car and walk to the back of it. As I did, he said without missing a beat, "What's wrong with your leg?"

I answered, with a bit more attitude than is advisable in such a situation and a smirk on my face, "I only got one."

The officer explained to me that I wouldn't be able to do all of the regular exercises in a field sobriety test. So instead he had me counting on my fingers, forward and backward—one, two, three, four, four, three, two, one. I found this all to be pretty annoying, so I turned to him and without thinking said, "We both know I'm drunk. Let's just do the Breathalyzer and get it over with."

He didn't have to say a word. His face read, "Oh crap." He didn't want to make me do it, but it was out there now. I blew my slightly boozy breath into that clear tube and registered just above the legal limit. I had given him no choice. He put me in the back of the cop car and then asked if I had any valuables in mine. "I have a few thousand dollars' worth of prosthetics in the trunk," I said.

When he called the wrecker he explained what was in the trunk. They actually parked it somewhere under a camera. I spent the night in a drunk tank.

When I made my court appearance the judge took pity on me.

"You do what I tell you, you will not have a DUI arrest on your permanent record," he said.

He then explained the rules. "For the next three months, here is your color. Your color is lime green. You call this number every day. And you're going to hear a recording with a list of colors, and if your color is one of them, you'll go to the location they tell you in Shelby County and you'll pay twenty-five dollars. Give them a urine sample and they will make sure you're not doing drugs or drinking."

The deal was I never knew when my color would come up. They make it so you can't clean out your system or try to time your drinking. It's totally random. My color, lime green, didn't come up very often. Midway through my three months I had another court date to check in with the judge. I had been lax for about a week and a half and just didn't call. I wasn't drinking. I just didn't call. I really don't know what I was thinking. I was being really stupid. But I guess it really shows where my head was back then. I didn't care what happened to me.

I arrived in court for my check-in and only half-tried to be serious. I was wearing blue jeans and a button-down shirt, untucked, with sleeves rolled to my forearms. The judge read through my paperwork and said, "You missed your color. Twice." He looked up at me like he didn't believe what he was reading. I just looked at him and calmly said, "There is no excuse, your honor."

He was furious. He had done me a huge favor and I just brushed it off. And I wasn't even upset about it. I think this made him even angrier. But that was it. He was done with being generous.

"Ten days in the county jail. No bail. No bond," he barked.

"Yes, sir."

He had given me a chance to make it right, to clear this from my record, but I hadn't taken it. I basically spat on his compassion and was nonchalant about it. He couldn't believe I didn't hold up my very easy end of the bargain. And now I was going to jail.

I knew I'd screwed up. I knew I was guilty, and I didn't care. I was living under the fog of this oppressive depression and nothing mattered. I am embarrassed about it now. Driving under the influence is not just putting myself at risk. I had put other lives at risk. I should have known better. I did know better.

I was taken straight from the courtroom and put on a bus with several other men and taken to county jail. A friend had come with me to my court date, so I just said to him, "Tell Tracy I'll be in county for ten days."

As we were loaded on the bus everyone was handcuffed but me. I couldn't be. My court appearance had been at night so it was late by the time we made it to the jail. In-processing took forever, too. That was particularly eventful for me, given that I wear prosthetics. Back then I was wearing a prosthetic arm as well as a leg. I never used the arm, but I wore it to help my clothes hang correctly. The arm I was wearing had a hook on the end, so I knew that wasn't coming with me to jail. I was standing at a window facing a guard on the other side as I signed all of the paperwork, took things out of my pockets, and then held up my arm and asked, "What do you want me to do with this?"

He looked a little bewildered and answered, "Um, can you take off the hook?"

"You can have the entire arm. I don't need it," I said.

"Oh, okay, then that's what we'll do." He seemed relieved that I'd solved the issue.

"Yeah, as long as I can keep my leg, I'm fine." I smiled.

A deputy sheriff led me into the next room for my strip search and he looked very confused. As I took my clothes off I could see him looking at my leg, not really sure how to handle it.

"Do you want me to take it off?" I asked.

"Yeah, yeah, take it off." He clearly didn't know what to do or say.

I stood on one leg and then slid off my leg and handed it to him. He took it and kind of just looked at it.

"You're good." He handed my leg back to me. I put it back on and pulled on my orange jumpsuit.

We all formed a line and filed through to receive our mattress, blanket, and pillow and head to our cell block, which was a large, open rectangular space with two levels of cells lining the walls. My cell was on the bottom, in a corner. There weren't bars, like the prison cells I'd seen in the movies. Instead the walls that faced out to the common area were bulletproof glass with a door made of more bulletproof glass. It was like being in a big fishbowl.

The guard opened my cell and I walked in to find a guy asleep on the bottom bunk. The door closed with a loud clank. The beds were steel-framed and bolted to the wall. The top bunk was really high. I looked up and thought, *I am not climbing all the way up there.* I just dropped my mattress on the floor and lay down. I didn't know who the other guy in the cell was or how he would react when he woke up. I was going to have to tell him he needed to take the top bunk and I was a little nervous about it. What was this guy in for exactly?

As soon as I dozed off, lights went on and it was morning. A guard came by and said something about me being down on the floor and he just looked at my cellmate and said, "You gotta go on top." The guy just said "okay" and put his stuff on top, and I put my mattress on the bottom bed.

We walked out to the common area in the middle for breakfast. Breakfast was runny fake eggs, flavorless grits, and a hard biscuit. No flavor and all a bland shade of off-white except for the tiny cup of watered-down Kool-Aid. But I discovered the longer you're in there, the sweeter that Kool-Aid tastes. You look forward to that tiny cup of pale pink sugary goodness.

We all crammed onto steel benches around three long tables, all bolted to the floor, and began to eat. A big, burly white guy covered in tattoos stood up at the other end of the table. As he walked toward me I could see that his eyes were slightly crossed. He stopped in front of the guy sitting next to me, my cellmate, and snapped, "Let me get that." He grabbed the guy's biscuit. I looked down at the floor and told myself, *Don't say anything. As long as he's not taking your food, don't get involved. Do not be a hero. Stay in your lane.*

After he devoured the biscuit he grabbed the guy's Kool-Aid and downed it in one swallow. He threw the cup down and went back to his seat. He then finished his own breakfast. I didn't say anything. No one said anything. We finished eating breakfast and headed back to our cells. We were in our cells for about an hour when they opened the doors and we got a little free time in the common area.

Guys were sitting around playing cards or talking or watching the communal TVs. It was December, so even within the walls of this jail it was obvious that it was chilly outside. But drawing on my only references for jail time, movies, and TV shows, I asked, "Hey, don't we get like an hour in the yard?"

After they finished laughing, the other guys told me, "It's not really outside. It's a room like this but there isn't a roof. Just a gate and a basketball hoop. It's cold."

I said, "Yeah, well that would still be a cool experience."

The guys all looked at me like I was crazy. But one of them went over to the intercom to ask the guards, "Are we going to get an hour on the court today?" The guard told him to hold on. A little while later the guard came over and asked, "Okay, who wants to go play some basketball?" No one volunteered until one of them said, "Noah, didn't you want to go?" I jumped up and said, "Yeah!" One of the other guys piped up and said he'd go with me. We were escorted to this big open-air circular room with a guard station in the middle and the sky above. There were cameras everywhere.

The guy who came with me was pretty unthreatening look-ing, about five foot eight, blond hair with a slight receding hair-line. We took a walk around and I saw that the basketball hoop was really just a raggedy old rim and down below it on the ground was a half-deflated basketball. As we walked around I noticed that there was writing all over the walls. It looked like it had been done with a paintbrush. I turned to the other inmate and asked, "What's this?"

"You take a pen, you break it open, and you use the ink to write. When the next cell block comes in, they can respond underneath." So then I walked around the room and read through several of these conversations. It was like a low-tech chat room or text messaging. It blew my mind because it was so inventive. The prisoners had figured out a way to communicate with people they never met. From what I remember, none of what they wrote was about beating up on guys and things like that as in the movies. It just seemed, for the most part, a way to stay connected to peo-ple, a basic human experience they were holding on to any way they could.

As I walked around the court with my new friend I realized I didn't even know his name yet.

"Hey, what's your name?"

"Michael Bolton," he replied.

"WHAT?!" I shouted.

"Yeah, I know. It's really Michael Bolton."

"Well I'll be damned. It's nice to meet you, Michael Bolton."

We spent a little while just talking and I asked him about his story. He told me about his girlfriend, who was in the same jail. She was in the women's unit in the next cell block. They had figured out how to pass notes back and forth through the air vent system. He was in for some sort of breaking-and-entering offense, although he seemed like a harmless guy. However I'm not really sure about that because he didn't tell me the full story.

After about an hour the guard came to get us and brought us back to our cell block. The other guys were playfully ragging on me. They asked me if I had enjoyed it. I said that I had and they all looked at me like I was ridiculous. But no one called me an idiot or threatened me.

As I started to feel more comfortable, I wanted to get to know these guys. I asked each of them to tell me his story. One of the guys cracked, "What's with all the questions? Are you writing a book?" I said, "Who knows? I might write a book sometime and talk about all of this." But for now I was curious. Some of them were super-intelligent, too smart for their own good. Others were as dumb as a box of rocks. In this way it did feel like a movie.

Maybe it was a bad upbringing that caused them not to use their brains for positive things. Instead they did bad things and got caught. Then there were the guys who did stupid things, got in trouble, and never found their way out of it. Their crimes got worse and worse and they dug themselves into deeper and deeper holes. There were a lot of repeat offenders, who felt trapped. They wanted to do better, but they had no help figuring out how to do that. If you go from the county to the penitentiary and spend some time there and then get out, you are not going to find a decent job. You're not going to make enough money to support your family and start over. Some people manage to pick up the pieces and move on. But that is the exception. Most of the time, that just doesn't happen. It's not uncommon for a person to get out of prison after several years, only to find himself in one dead-end job after another. They come to believe it's easier to be in prison than out in the real world and struggling. So they get this mentality of *I don't care what happens to me.*

Talking to these men and hearing their stories made me realize that while I was struggling with some demons, I was not in their place. I was serving ten days for a DUI. Thankfully I had not harmed anyone as a result of my careless actions. I had not committed a serious crime. I was still capable of being saved. I could pull myself out of this path. This was another spark of that wake-up call I really needed. I just thought, *I do not need to end up back here. I can't end up back here.*

Hearing these stories made me realize how easily I could fall into this trap and not get myself out. I was worried, thinking, *Is this going to be me someday? Is this who I've become? This bitter veteran who finds himself in trouble all the time?*

Another thing I learned about these guys was that a lot of them had kids. They almost never saw their kids, however. And I sat there thinking, *No way. I love my children. I cannot be taken away from them forever. I cannot allow this to happen to me. I have to turn it around.* If not for me, for Colston, Jack, and Rian. A lot of these guys in here had fathers who were incarcerated. They followed in their fathers' footsteps. That terrified me. I don't want my kids to grow up with a parent like that, an example like that to follow.

After our morning free time we went back into our cells until lunch. The trays came back out to those three tables in the middle of the common room. We never left the block or saw any other inmates. After lunch there was another lockdown period in our

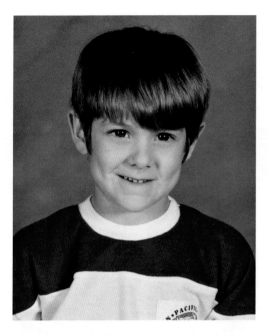

ABOVE: Here is my all-American obligatory class picture.

ABOVE: Proof I had an early career in baseball during second grade.

ABOVE: The Siblings Galloway. (*Clockwise from right*) Jennifer, Sara, Katherine and me.

Above left: This is the Army's version of class picture day, taken during Basic Training in 2001. Above right: (*Top*) My grandpa, Andrew Colston Galloway Sr., came to welcome me home from my first deployment in 2004. (*bottom*) My sister Jennifer, and my nieces, Alex and Abby, welcomed me home from my first deployment to Iraq in 2004.

Above: This is how my platoon caught some shut-eye in the war zone. We were not living in camps, we were constantly moving forward, fighting the enemy.

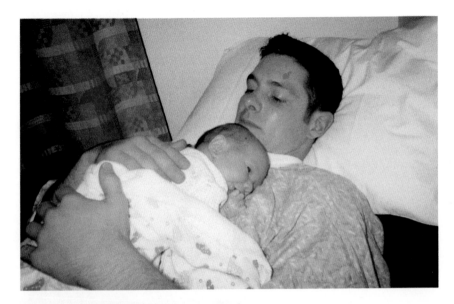

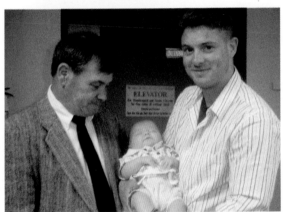

ABOVE: Colston was born with a serious medical condition that kept us in the hospital in Nashville for three months while he received specialized care. LEFT: After spending his first three months in a children's hospital in Nashville, Colston finally came home to Alabama. My dad, Andy Galloway, was one proud grandfather.

RIGHT: Nothing compares to fatherhood. Here with my oldest boy, Colston, before I left for my second deployment.

ABOVE: Here I am with my platoon leader Jerry Eidson and buddy Regis, who is photobombing. We are holding up one of the Motorola pagers the enemy used to detonate bombs.

ABOVE: Action shot. GI Joes in real life.

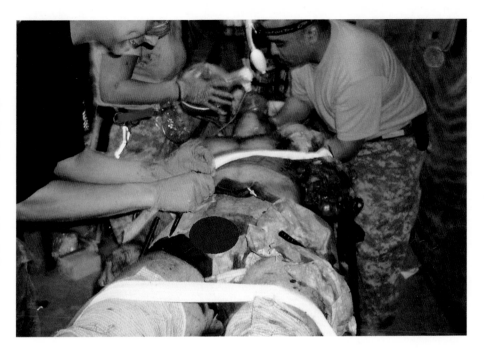

Above: The crucial moments after the explosion and the incredible medical team that worked fiercely to save my life.

Above: What was left of our Humvee after it was pulled out of the canal, long after I had been rescued. Notice the water line and blood still visible even after all that time.

OPPOSITE ABOVE: Trying to look like I know what I'm doing on *Dancing with the Stars* with my stunning partner, Sharna Burgess. OPPOSITE BELOW: Sharna and I definitely became known for our lifts on the 20th Anniversary Season of *Dancing with the Stars*. ABOVE: My serious face for the headshots of Fox's *American Grit*.

ABOVE: A little fun-in-the-sun time with my kids.
(*From left to right*) Jack, Rian, me and Colston. *All photos
(except as noted) are from the author's personal collection.*

cells before another period of free time, another lockdown, dinner, and final lights-out lockdown.

There was a TV mounted way up on the wall, too high to reach, but everyone could see it from their cells. We were allowed to go up to the intercom and request a channel four times a day. The guard would eventually change the channel but never right away. You had to know what number corresponded with which channel you wanted. Like channel twenty-one is Syfy or channel twenty-three is ABC. Whatever it was, you had to know the number. There was no guide.

One afternoon four guys, two older and two younger, started bickering about what to watch on TV. The argument went on and on, until I couldn't take it anymore.

"Listen, we've watched *Bonanza* all goddamn morning. It's only fair that if these guys want to watch the Syfy channel they watch it in the afternoon. And then before we go to dinner, we can put it on the local station, so when we go to lockdown we can watch the local news before they shut everything down," I snapped.

They all just kind of stood there and looked at each other. Finally one of them said, "That's fair. All right." So that's what happened. They changed it to Syfy, and around dinner they asked to change it to the local channel, so we watched the news and went to sleep. By coming up with a plan, I had gained a little respect.

If you're in jail long enough you are provided with a commissary account. Friends and family can add money to your account. Every Thursday the guys who worked in the commissary would come by with a sheet of paper that had a list of their inventory—snacks, playing cards, and things like that. You marked off what you wanted and then you turned in your request. A few days later they brought you the items you requested and subtracted the price from the total of your account. It's almost exactly like in *Orange Is the New Black,* only they come to you instead of your going to a little window.

After I'd been in a few days I learned a little more information about my quiet cellmate, whose name was Ed. After that first night he moved up to the top bunk without incident. Whenever we were on lockdown it was just the two of us in there and I kept trying to make conversation with the guy. As I'm sure is clear by now, I'm a talker.

He appeared to be a little older than me, I'd guess around his mid-forties. So I talked and talked, but it just seemed like the words weren't even registering with him. He could speak but it was obvious that he wasn't really getting what I was saying. Something was definitely off about him. He never made eye contact. He was always looking off somewhere in the distance. He always acted very nervous and unsure of himself. He almost seemed like a child trapped in a man's body. Whenever we had time to be out in the common area, he stayed in our cell. He only came out for meals. I was determined to get this guy talking. Whenever we'd go to lockdown I was in there peppering him with questions in a friendly manner. I asked, "What are you here for?" All I got out of that question was, "Ever since that day. Ever since that day everything went downhill." I regretted asking him that question and thought, *Oh man, this guy killed somebody. I am going to have to sleep with one eye open!*

This balding, middle-aged man-child just sat there, looking nonthreatening. He had a pretty good belly on him. And his mannerisms struck me as childlike. He was always talking about his mom. In his mutterings about "that day" he also said, "I just wanna get back to my mom." At first glance I didn't find him threatening, but all this talk had me thinking he was like Norman Bates from *Psycho* and maybe he had killed his mother. But then he said, "Ever since that day when I turned two, my parents didn't want me anymore."

When he said that I found myself thinking, *I'd rather he had told me he killed someone. This is much, much creepier.* It was clear my cellmate was not right in the head. I asked the other guys about him and they all said the same thing.

"He shouldn't be here. He's not mentally stable. This is jail, not a psych ward. It's wrong that they have him here. He's been here for over nine months."

I was really taken aback that all of these tough criminals agreed and were standing up for this guy.

If Ed went to court, every man in this cell block would have testified in his defense, saying he was mentally challenged. They felt sympathy for him and it bothered them all that he was in that environment. It almost seemed as if they were more concerned about him than about their own issues.

I realized I couldn't really talk to him, but I watched him to learn more. When the commissary guys came around, I never ordered anything, because I wasn't going to be there long enough to worry about it. But my cellmate got a regular delivery. He ordered a couple of sleeves of flower-shaped cookies with cream filling. This made perfect sense to me. If you're a child and somewhere scary and they ask you what you'd like as a treat, of course you'll ask for cookies. Other guys got snacks like honey buns or potato chips but he always got cookies, and the kind you might find served in a kindergarten for snack time.

One afternoon I decided to play cards with some of the guys. But I noticed that the big burly guy, Bubba, who stole food as he pleased, had wandered into my cell. I was sitting with three other guys at a table, and from my seat I could see straight into my cell. As the guy across from me was dealing the cards and his back was to my cell, I said, "What's Bubba doing in my cell?"

The guy across from me turned and glanced around before saying, "I don't know."

"I think he's eating my cellmate's cookies," I said.

The other guy kept dealing cards. The gears in my brain were turning furiously. It's not like you could talk to my cellmate. He was not capable of real conversation. So he was not capable of saying, "Yes, you may have some of my cookies." It's clear that Bubba just went in there and took the cookies and was eating them right in front of him, taking advantage of this mentally deficient guy.

That was it. I couldn't handle it. "This is some bullshit," I said as I smacked my cards down onto the table and walked into my cell to confront this cell block bully.

"What are you doing?" I asked.

"Man, we're just in here talking," he said.

"Bullshit. You're eating his fucking cookies."

"Aw, man, I haven't touched his cookies."

"You'd better not or I am gonna whoop your ass," I said defiantly. And then I walked out and sat back down at the table and stared straight into the cell. The big guy was facing my bunk so I was looking at him from the side. I just glared at his profile. He stood there, not turning his head even an inch to catch my eye. Finally he walked out and went back to his cell.

I continued playing cards until afternoon lockdown. When the doors opened for dinner we all walked out and grabbed our trays. I looked around and realized the big guy wasn't there. He hadn't come out of his cell for dinner.

My head filled with absolute dread. I thought, *Oh man, what have I done? I'm only here for ten days. He's probably making some homemade shank, so he can stab me.* He was top dog in there and I disrespected him. Why did I feel I had to protect people? I needed to do my ten days and go home. That's it. I didn't need to do anything else. This wasn't summer camp. I had to quit sticking my nose in other people's business.

He never came out for dinner, and nothing happened. We went back for lockdown. We sat in our cells, we watched the news, because my perfect plan for shared TV use was working, and we sat there at our glass walls and watched the news from our cells until bedtime.

The next morning at breakfast the big guy reemerged. I told myself not to worry and not to start anything. I hoped he had gotten a little rest and had calmed down. We were sitting there eating and suddenly old burly got up and walked toward my table. I was sitting next to Ed the way I did for every meal. As soon as Bubba got close enough, my cellmate covered his tray with his hands and shouted, "NO! You ain't getting it today!" He slid his Kool-Aid to me.

My immediate thought was, *Do not touch that Kool-Aid, Noah. You don't want to get in the middle of this.* So what did I do? I touched the Kool-Aid. Well, then the guy across from me slid me his Kool-Aid. I looked up and Bubba was still standing in front of me. I stared him down. He was pissed but he finally sulked off back to his seat. From there on out I had three Kool-Aids to drink. And they all offered me their food, too.

On the third afternoon of my jail time, I sat down to play solitaire. One of the guys shouted over, "Hey, Noah, what are we going to watch today? What should we choose?" I looked up a little annoyed and responded, "Aw man, I don't care."

The guy looked at me a little dumbfounded and said, "Well, we don't know what to watch."

"Man, I don't care. I'm playing solitaire. I'm not even watching TV. Choose whatever you want."

The guy walked off back to the group to contemplate this very difficult decision he appeared to not be able to make without me. It was ridiculous. I just shook my head and thought, *I'm playing solitaire, don't mess me up.*

I kept playing my game and one of the other guys walked over to talk to me. I had gotten to know several of these guys over the last few days, learning their stories, where they came from, and how they got here. This was one of the younger guys, an African-American in his twenties. Let's call him Jamal. He started talking to me and opened up about his childhood. His parents died at a young age and he spent his youth in and out of juvenile detention centers. This led to him getting into bigger trouble as an adult. I told him, "Man, I've done some speaking at schools through this foundation called Lakeshore. And I'll tell you, your experiences, they could help people. With your background, your childhood, there are some kids going through the same things you did."

He nodded in agreement and said, "I know. I know they are."

"If you could clean up your act and go out and share your experiences with kids, you could really explain how bad choices can lead to even worse circumstances like jail time. Maybe you'll be the wake-up call they need. I can't talk about that. I'm spending ten days in the county. I haven't been to juvy. I haven't grown up without parents. I haven't had the experiences that you have. You could really reach out to kids going through these kinds of things. This could be a new path for you."

He looked at me with a glimmer of hope in his eye. "Do you really think so?" he asked.

"Yes, I do. Life is all about just using what you have and making it work for you."

It's funny, because as I was telling him this I knew I had the recipe for success and the solution to my own problems. As I explained this new path to him I was also learning about myself and that I needed to change my life.

This was another example of seeing how stuck these people were. I realized that I was going through a little divot. I wasn't stuck yet.

You learn so much when you show someone else. And that's what I was experiencing.

I had dropped out of school just a few weeks into the ninth grade. I hated school because I felt I was just being talked at. I wasn't being taught. I know now that I learn differently from others. Don't tell me, show me, let me experience it hands-on and have to tell someone else how to do it. Then I will learn.

Suddenly all of that sank in for me. I was talking to these guys, helping them work through their issues and giving them my thoughts on where I think they could go from here. I was explaining the positive possibilities to them and simultaneously realizing that the same could be true for me—good or bad. In that brief ten-day period, I went through some massive changes.

The last night I was there, Jamal called me over into his cell. He pulled out a cardboard box from under his bunk. The box was full of snacks that he had bought from the commissary. There were potato chips, dill pickle chips, salt and vinegar chips, some honey buns, and Doritos.

He held the box out toward me and said, "Take one." I said, "Nah, man, I'm leaving tomorrow. I can get McDonald's tomorrow if I want to. I probably will. I'm not going to take your snacks. You keep them."

"No, man, I want you to take something," he insisted. I recognized that this was his way of thanking me. It was all he had to offer. Moved by the gesture, I took a bag of salt and vinegar chips. I walked back to my cell and sat there on my bunk and ate those chips thinking, *Noah, what are you going to take away from all of this? What are you going to do to change? You have been telling these guys all week what they should do. You earned their respect, but what if one day you run across one of these guys again? Are you going to look like you're full of it because your life is still a mess? What if you've done nothing with your life five years from now?* I sat there thinking about it as I crunched on those chips with the local news reporters chattering along from the overhead TV until lights-out.

I woke up the next day for my last incarcerated morning, pulled out my cards, and started playing solitaire to pass the time until I was released. I waited all day. I mean, we had breakfast and lunch and I was still waiting. I was just beginning to wonder how long I would have to wait when finally a guard sauntered up and said, "Galloway, get your stuff, get your bed." I ran to my cell to get my stuff and I grabbed the toothpaste. The toothpaste was in this clear tube and was clear like hair gel. It had a muted, watered-down mint flavor. Everything you got in jail was made specifically to be as safe as can be. One of the guys told me, "Don't ever take anything from being locked up. It's bad luck." But I told myself, *You ain't coming back. You ain't getting locked up again, so you're taking a souvenir.* I grabbed that little clear tube and I put it in my pocket and walked out of my cell. As I came out, all of the guys from my cellblock were lined up to say goodbye. The guard had this look on his face like, "What is going on?" I walked down the line shaking each man's hands. They all told me they were glad they had met me. They told me that I made an impact on them. One guy said, "You came in here and you've been to war and back, you're missing two limbs, but you still had a smile on your face the whole time. You've gone through so much and you are able to keep smiling. That motivates me." I was really touched.

I kept going down the line, shaking hands and saying my fare-wells, and finally I got to Michael Bolton. He said, "Hey, man, I've asked people this before and they never follow through with it but I believe you will. Could you print out some TV guides? Because you know we just tell them the number. We don't know what's on at what time, what station." I said, "Yeah, man, I'll do that." And I looked around to the other guys and asked, "Does anybody want any crossword puzzles or anything like that?" They all said that would be awesome.

"All right, Michael, I've got your address so I'm gonna send it to you. And listen, man, I'm gonna give you my email address.

When you get out shoot me an email. I want to stay in touch and see how things are going."

I turned to the guard who was still baffled by what was happening and said, "I'm ready." He rolled his eyes and opened the door. We walked out and they handed me my clothes. I pulled off the orange jumpsuit and tossed it. I changed back into my clothes. I signed everything I had to sign, got some paperwork to take with me, and walked out a free man again.

Well, my epic freedom moment was short-lived, because I realized my cell phone was dead. I walked down the road to a gas station and asked if I could use the phone. I called Tracy and told her where I was and asked her to pick me up. When Tracy arrived I hopped in the car and the very first thing I said to her was "I gotta get home. I have to print out some TV guides and I need to write a letter to some of the guys in there." She started laughing and when she could compose herself enough to talk said, "My sisters and I all said we guarantee Noah is going to come out of jail with new friends. He's going to be friends with everybody."

I got home and immediately wrote a letter to Michael Bolton. I put my email address at the bottom. I printed out TV guides. I printed out crossword puzzles. I even printed a couple of pages of jokes and riddles and whatever would be fun to read and do and folded them up and put them in an envelope. All that was left to do was to write the address, put a stamp on the envelope, and put it in the mailbox. I put the envelope in the car in between the seat and the center console to take to the post office.

I must have been distracted or had to do something else because the envelope sat there for months. Every so often I would look at it and go, *Oh crap, I haven't sent that yet.* And then at some point I spilled something on it so I knew I would never send it now. I threw it out.

To this day I'm worried that one day I'm going to be at the gas station in line and hear a voice behind me say, "I'm Michael Bolton and you never sent me my damn TV guide. You're just like the rest." He's going to shank me in my side and that will be the end of the Noah Galloway story.

CHAPTER 15

Final Kick in
the Pants

(2010)

THIS IS WHERE I need to point out again that my life is not a Hollywood story. In a movie, I would have learned my lesson in jail, snapped out of my depression, and stopped behaving badly because I'd seen the light. Well, that was not my reality. My life is not a movie. At least not yet.

It wasn't long before I was back to my old ways. The lessons I'd learned were quickly fading into the background and I was out drinking as often as possible. Tracy was struggling through postpartum depression, so Jack and Rian were spending a lot of time at Tracy's mom's house. Tracy and I weren't helping each other at all. This meant I was free of responsibility and had nothing better to do, so I started to hang out at a Japanese steak house near our home. I would sit at the bar and drink sake and eat sushi for hours by myself. I ordered the same thing every time. It was a roll that wasn't even on the menu but it became the Noah roll: tuna, cream cheese, and jalapeños.

I befriended the people who worked at the steak house. Funnily enough, not one of them was Japanese. They were a Chinese family, who started to invite me over to drink with them after the restaurant closed. They told me they'd never had a white person in their house before. I was even invited to celebrate Chinese New Year with them and eat their home-cooked, traditional food. I was forming an alcohol-infused bond with this family while I neglected my own.

On Christmas Eve, Tracy put the kids to bed and I told her that I was going out with my friends from the steak house for a while and that when I got home, we'd set up Christmas for the kids. She said all right. What else was she going to say at this point? We both had given up making an effort. But she said to wake her when I got home and we'd set up all of the gifts together for the kids.

I met up with those guys and, boy, could they drink. We drank and drank and drank and drank. Finally I poured myself into my car and drove the short distance home, once again putting others in danger. But I wasn't thinking about any consequences at all. I remember getting home and stumbling my way to the front door. I fell over, but I caught myself with my one arm. As I crouched there, propped up on my right arm and leg, I just started puking all over the front walk. In between heaves and gasps, all I was thinking was, *Do not ruin Christmas for the kids. Do not ruin Christmas for the kids.*

I managed to pull myself together, wipe the vomit off my face, and get into the house. Luckily, I didn't wake Tracy. I didn't want her to see me like that.

I got all of the presents and put them under the tree by myself. Then it was all I could do to find my way to the couch, where I passed out. I woke up on Christmas morning and my first thought was, *Holy shit, this is exactly the kind of father I said I would never be.* I realized what a horrible example I was setting. This was another shove in the right direction, but it would take more to really kick me into gear to make a real change.

Soon after Christmas my cousin Corey came to talk to me. He'd been dealing with a few different minor health issues that caused him to get out of shape. He came to me to ask some questions and get my advice about getting fit again.

His visit made me feel I was worth something, that I had something to offer. So I talked to Corey and gave him some advice, and then I was off and running on a project. I had a mission. I started spending my time on the computer looking up information for Corey instead of spending it at the steak house or anywhere else getting drunk.

I suggested that Corey and I start working out together. And this time I went to Eric. He didn't need to convince me again. I was ready now. So he paid for my membership to a twenty-four-hour gym. But before I could really start helping Corey, I needed to figure out myself. I needed to relearn how to work out and what would work best for my new body, but I didn't want to do that when there were a lot of people around.

There was no way I could get Corey back into shape if I wasn't in shape myself. So I started going to the gym by myself at 2 a.m. I could use the machines to work my right side but I had to experiment and figure out how to work my left side. Then I realized I could use an ankle strap, put it on the residual limb on my arm, hook it to a cable machine, and have the resistance on my chest. I could then turn sideways, lower the cable, and lift up from the shoulder using my deltoid. I could lift back up, level with the machine facing me, and pull back to work my back. I was finding all kinds of ways to use that strap to work my injured side. I was making the best of what I had and making it work. I figured out how to work my whole body and I saw a path to getting back into the kind of shape I was used to. For the first time that goal seemed reachable.

I also changed the way I was eating. I got Corey eating a healthier diet, too. And now that I was ready, I started working out with Corey in the afternoon, after he left work. I no longer minded if people saw me. I wasn't embarrassed. I was getting stronger every day. And I was packing on muscle. I felt great for the first time in a very long time. I had more energy for my kids and that felt incredibly good. I knew I was finally on the right track.

I've had people all my life telling me, "You've got it, use it." That doesn't motivate me. If it's just for me, I lose interest. I don't see the benefit. For me to see the purpose of what I do I need to see that it affects other people.

I continued to work out every day. It became my job and I became obsessed. I even started working out at an even bigger gym because it was almost like an ego stroke to have more people see what I could do instead of having them just stare at the two limbs missing from my body. My motivation directly stemmed from, and is still directly connected to, my ability to motivate others with my actions. And I finally woke up to realize that I'd better make sure those actions were positive ones, especially for my most important audience—my three children.

So it wasn't the movie version. I didn't see the light and fix myself immediately after going to jail, or after throwing up on my front porch on Christmas Eve, or just because of Corey. But all three of those things had to happen and build on each other in order for me to finally get the point. So, as I said, this isn't a movie and I am a flawed character but I'm just trying to give it to you straight. This is how it happened.

CHAPTER 16

———

Tornadoes and Terrorists

APRIL 27, 2011, brought one of the worst tornado outbreaks in Alabama's history. Sixty-two tornadoes ripped through Alabama and destroyed much of the state. Two hundred and fifty-two people died and thousands were left without homes. I remember that day as clearly as I remember September 11, 2001.

Growing up in Alabama, I was used to tornadoes. I knew to take the warnings and watches seriously.

I had the news on and was watching the coverage when the cameras caught the first one live on air. I was standing in front of my TV watching live as a tornado ripped through Tuscaloosa, which is where Colston was living with his mother. Gripping my phone and hitting redial on both Brandi's and her parents' phone numbers, I watched in horror as the massive funnel cloud barreled its way through town. I couldn't get anyone to answer the phone and all I could think was, *Am I watching my son die?*

I was terrified. Finally the storm ended and I got a hold of Colston's granddad. He told me they were all fine. Relief washed over me. But not for long. Another tornado popped up right after the first one and wreaked havoc all over the region. By the time the skies finally settled, there was severe damage all the way from Tuscaloosa through northwest Georgia.

The next day as I watched the news, I saw the devastation and grief and felt an overwhelming need to help. I didn't know what to do, but I had to do something. I'd been working out fairly regularly by this point and was in good enough shape to feel I could be of help.

I called some friends who said they were going to Ashville, Alabama. My parents lived there for a while, on a street that was in a valley. My dad always said that if a tornado ever hit there, it would destroy everything in that valley, and that's exactly what happened. The tornado crisscrossed through like a pinball, leaving many houses flattened and some not touched at all. We went to help an elderly woman who couldn't leave her home. We came with chain saws and cut trees and cleared the driveway.

The next day I went to Bessemer, Alabama, on my own. Before I had been with a group of friends. No one questioned what I was capable of doing. But now I was on my own. I didn't know how people would react to a guy with one arm and one leg. I was afraid I'd be asked to just take donations. But no one ever questioned me.

Over the following days, my friends and I signed waivers, boarded buses, and headed out to various communities. We went house to house asking if anyone needed help. We put tarps on roofs, cleaned up debris in the streets and out of homes—we did anything the survivors needed us to do.

I went back every day for two weeks, working from sunup to sundown. Each day I was out looking for groups to volunteer with and people to help. As I drove through the small town of Hueytown I saw a bus parked outside a church with a sign that said DISASTER RELIEF. I pulled over and went inside.

"What can I do? I'm here to work."

I don't know if any of them were actually questioning me, but I felt like I was getting a few looks that said, "How can this guy help? He is missing an arm and a leg." As I was standing there the weather was starting to turn. I could see the rain was coming as a guy pulled up in a truck. "Man, I need some tarps. My roof was blown off and that rain is coming," he said.

There was another guy standing there beside me and we both said without hesitation that we would help. We packed up some tarps and followed the man to a town called Pleasant Grove. I have cousins who live there, but I hadn't driven through since before the tornado. It was unrecognizable. Houses were gone, cars were upside down and scattered all over the place. It looked like a war zone. And I would know.

We arrived at the man's house and got to work. I started to feel much more confident and less self-conscious. I was working away at getting nails into this tarp on the side of the roof as quickly as I could. *Bam, bam, bam, WHOOSH!* All of a sudden I dropped the hammer and down it went, disappearing into the debris two floors down. That hammer was now in the middle of two entire floors of partially collapsed home. Everything was down there, including the kitchen sink, which was poking up out of the pile. But the guy seemed really upset about the hammer and scurried down off the roof to look for it. I felt bad, but thought, *It's just a hammer.*

We kept working and finished attaching the tarp. Thankfully everyone else had a hammer, and I helped to hold down tarps or hold down nails. Then we went to help look for the hammer that fell. We got down to the pile of rubble, and I could see that the man was really upset. He was waist-high in junk, throwing bits and pieces of his life all over the place, digging for this tool. He saw us and said, "It was my dad's hammer. He was a carpenter and he passed away a little while ago." My heart sank.

I could see that the big thing was not that I had lost his dead dad's hammer; it was that this man had lost *everything.* I immediately started looking. He saw what I was doing and said, "Don't worry about it, man, you'll get hurt trying to do that." I waved him off and told him I was just going to have a look. I scoured the enormous pile of debris that had been a house and was just about to give up when a glint of something metallic caught my eye. I got a little closer and saw that, hanging right in the middle of a bush was the hammer. I ran over and grabbed it and gave it back to its happy owner.

I showed up the next day and the next to work with the volunteers. I viewed this as my new job. I went every day for several weeks. I felt great because I had purpose again. I was getting up early in the morning, working hard all day, and getting home late. It was also the first time since I was injured that I was doing manual labor. This too felt amazing, because there is nothing better than instant gratification and manual labor provides just that. I could see just how much debris I cleared or how many tarps I helped to put on roofs. It was invigorating to get up early, put on my boots, work until the sun went down, come home, eat dinner, pass out, and do it all again the next day. I loved it. And I loved knowing that what I was doing was directly contributing to making things better for the people whose lives had been ripped up and thrown upside down. There was something deeply satisfying in that. I was once again able to serve and protect, just in a different way.

After another long day of disaster relief work, and knowing I had to be up early for more, I was getting ready for bed but decided I'd check Facebook first. This was well before I was as up-to-date on social media as I am now. I wasn't checking it all the time. But on a whim, I decided to take a quick peek on my laptop. The first thing I saw in my news feed was "Osama bin Laden is dead." I kept scrolling through my feed but every post was the same thing. Then I read a post that said, "The president is about to speak." I flipped on the TV, but President Obama hadn't even made it to the podium yet. That's how fast news was traveling on social media. Then Obama walked into frame and I, along with the rest of the world, heard him say the words we'd all been waiting ten years to hear.

"Tonight, I can report to the American people and to the world that the United States has conducted an operation that killed Osama bin Laden, the leader of al Qaeda, and a terrorist who's responsible for the murder of thousands of innocent men, women, and children."

I couldn't believe it. I felt joy, shock, excitement, and an over-whelming pride about being an American. The news cut to scenes of other Americans cheering in the streets. This was an awesome, fist-pump, proud-to-be-an-American moment.

My phone pinged with a text message from an old friend, Mandy Goff. She thanked me for my sacrifice, for all that I and all of the other veterans and soldiers had done that led to this moment. She told me that she loved and appreciated me. That text hit me hard. I think up to this point I still had a pretty high wall up around my emotions toward the war, including the reasons I was there and the reasons why I came home less whole than when I left. But Mandy's text tore a whole in that wall, and I completely broke down. I was sitting alone on the couch, nothing but the light of the television illuminating the room, and I was sobbing. Every emotion I felt that day and every day since just washed over me.

* * *

SEPTEMBER 11, 2001

Everyone says this, but it was just a normal Tuesday. I'd taken my GED and was just a few weeks into my first semester at University of Alabama at Birmingham. I was also working part-time at a vitamin supplement store in the mall. Brandi and I had been dating about a year and were recently engaged. That day I had the morning off from work and class, so I had spent the night at Brandi's house.

Brandi was at school and I was enjoying having the place to myself and was sleeping late. But I was jolted awake when the phone rang.

I remember grunting, exasperated that I'd been awakened, but I grabbed the phone and yelled, "HELLO?"

"Noah, it's me. Turn on the TV." It was my best friend Justin. He sounded panicked.

I grabbed the remote and turned on the TV. I didn't even have to ask what station. It was on every station. Smoke billowed out of one of the twin towers of the World Trade Center, in New York City. Dark, ash-gray smoke poured out of the building and polluted the perfectly cloudless, bright blue sky. The news anchors were saying things like, "We think it's pilot error." Everyone on the ground had their eyes on the towers.

And then I watched along with everyone on the scene as the second plane slammed into the second tower. It was a burst of flames and then you could hear the screams of those around the camera. The reporters were frantically talking live on-air in fragmented sentences, trying to figure out what just happened. And I was watching, shocked, confused, and in disbelief.

In a split second the nation went from thinking it was just tragic pilot error to knowing the United States of America was under attack. And then all you heard were the horrified screams of the people who were there. I watched for as long as I could. I probably sat glued to the TV for an hour. My head was foggy as the images played out in front of my face—buildings falling down, people running and screaming, the ash filling Manhattan. When I couldn't watch any more, I jumped up and turned the TV off. I threw on some shorts, a T-shirt, and sneakers and bolted out of the front door. I went for a run. I didn't have a plan or a route, I just ran. As I ran and ran I was thinking, I need to join the military. If there is military action, I need to do it.

I'd considered the military before. Most of my mom's side of the family had served in some capacity and she had tried for years to convince me to join. I even went so far as to go speak to a recruiter once. That was about a year before now. I originally thought I'd like to be a firefighter in the Air Force but I was told I couldn't apply without a high school education. I was advised to at least get my GED, which I did. But after passing the tests to achieve the GED, the women administering the testing urged me to apply to college. Brandi supported this as well because she wanted to keep me close to her. Once I got into college I didn't think about joining up again. But on September 11, 2001, everything changed. Now my country was under attack. We might go to war and I needed to be a part of that. My country needed me.

I just kept running until finally I stopped and realized I had run quite far from the house. And I was thirsty. I saw a gas station and headed that way. There were cars lined up all the way down the street to get gas. It looked like something out of a disaster movie. Everyone was freaking out. All of the people in the cars had the same terrified look on their faces.

I walked into the gas station convenience store, grabbed a Gatorade, and got in line. And then when I got to the counter I said the stupidest thing I could have said. The cashier was a Middle Eastern man and I said to him, "Business is good today, isn't it?"

He glared at me like I was the rudest, nastiest person on the planet. He didn't have to reply. His face said it all. Inside my head I was screaming, Why did you say that? *I was so distraught over what I'd seen on the TV, about what was happening to my country, I think I had pulled up my imaginary shield and gone into emotional protection mode. It's what I do when I am upset or uncomfortable.*

I paid for the Gatorade and drank the whole bottle before heading back to Brandi's house. When she came home I told her that I was joining up. We were newly engaged, but I wasn't going to discuss this. I had made up my mind. Within just a few days I was back at that recruitment station I had originally visited. The same recruiter was there and he remembered me. I walked in and said, "This is for real. I'm in. I want airborne and I want infantry." By October 1, 2001, my bags were packed and I was headed in a van to Fort Benning, Georgia, for basic training.

* * *

I sat in front of the TV for some time after learning of Bin Laden's death. By now the news was looping footage of the president's speech mixed with scenes from the attacks on 9/11. Bin Laden is the reason all those people lost their lives that day. His horrible actions are the reason so many of us joined the military. He is the reason I joined the military. He is the reason we went to war, why people lost their lives in combat, and he is the reason I lost two of my limbs. He was the big, bad, evil bogeyman behind all of this tragedy, and he was gone.

I was flooded with emotions, I was sobbing, but overall I was happy. I finally had validation for what had happened to me. Say what you will about why we went to war, this guy needed to go. We as a country needed that. I needed that. I think that this news also came at a critical time for me since I was coming out of my depression. It helped me turn the corner. It put to rest a huge thing that was on my mind when I didn't even realize it had been on my mind. His death was a critical part of my recovery because it happened as I was in the process. I was making a lot of positive changes. It was the biggest thing that happened in my recovery that directly had to do with the war. Ding, dong, the witch is dead.

CHAPTER 17

Let's Go Racing

MY RETURN TO FITNESS created even more tension between Tracy and me. I went from ignoring her because I was depressed to having no time for her because I was so obsessed with fitness. The feeling of being ships passing in the night only grew stronger. She would stay up late on the couch with Rian and Jack, and I would go to bed at 7 p.m., since I would be getting up to go to the gym at 4 a.m. I no longer cared what time I went or if Corey was there with me. I was just going as often as I could.

I was much more aware of what I was putting into my body, so while I still went out some, I was definitely not drinking myself into thoughtless oblivion. Drinking was the one thing Tracy and I were still doing together on occasion. One night we were out and one of our friends went to take a picture of us. I slid my beer away from me before they snapped the group shot. Later that night I sat my beer down for another picture. Tracy noticed and called me out.

"What, are you too good to have a beer in your hand now?" she asked.

"I'm working on something. That's not the image I want to represent me on social media," I responded.

I don't think I even realized fully at the time, but I was rebranding myself. I was creating the image of the man and father I wanted to become. I finally had found my new focus and purpose. Gone were pictures of drinking with friends, and in their place were status updates about my workouts. People began to notice. And in particular, my former platoon leader, Jerry Eidson, noticed. We had remained close friends through everything, so Jerry saw my posts, and he was happy to see them, but he wanted to make sure I stayed on the right course. He called to issue me a challenge.

"Hey, Noah, I see you're getting back into shape. There is a race north of Atlanta that I just heard about. Look it up. I don't know if you can do it, but if you can, I'd love to do it with you," he said.

I told him I would check it out and call him back. I looked it up online and found out it was a Warrior Dash 5K. People dress up to run the course full of easy obstacles and a lot of mud. It looked really fun. It was even a Scottish event, and the Galloways are Scottish. I called Jerry back immediately. I was all in on this!

"This is awesome. Let's do it! And if we do it, let's grow full beards and wear kilts. I'll find the kilts."

To date, this was the only time Jerry's wife let him grow a beard. We spent three months growing our beards and then showed up at this race in our kilts along with twenty thousand other people. I had Jerry there by my side to support me, but back in Birmingham, Eric was still supporting me. He paid my entry fee for this race. He knew how to encourage me without pushing me too far.

Jerry and I got out there on the course and it just about killed me. I'd been working out for size. My singular goal was to build muscle, so I had no endurance. We got out on the course and it kicked my butt. I tried to run and maneuver through the trails and found the obstacles were much more challenging than I anticipated. Jerry helped me where he could.

As we were nearing the end of this unexpectedly brutal course we rounded a corner to see a two-story wall. Just a bunch of slats of wood stacked on top of each other. The only help was that every so many feet there was a two-by-four sticking out as a thin ledge and there were ropes hanging down from the top to use to pull yourself up and over. Jerry and I stopped dead in our tracks and just stared up at it.

"How are you going to climb this?" he asked.

"I don't know, but we have to figure it out," I answered.

I took a deep breath and trotted forward to get a better look. That's when I noticed that this particular obstacle was in a bend in the course, and just off to the left was one of the places spectators gathered to watch and cheer on their friends. I grabbed the rope with one hand. I reach as high up on the rope as I could and I pulled all of my body weight up in a one-arm pull-up. I threw a leg up on the first two-by-four. I was able to right myself and get my footing without letting go of the rope. I carefully slid my hand up the rope and turned my head to yell for Jerry.

"Jerry! Hold the rope tightly. As I try to slide up, the rope wants to go in the same direction. Keep it taut."

Jerry did as I asked. He put his foot on the rope and held on to it. I slid my hand up and pulled my body weight up again and was able to get my foot on the next two-by-four. I got all the way to the top like that. When I reached the top and threw my upper body over the wall I heard a swell of cheers and applause from the crowd. What a rush! I fed off that energy and was fired up. I shimmied my way down the other side and Jerry and I made it to the finish line.

As the race ended, the party got started. They had a band, beer, and giant turkey legs. It was a really good time. I had my first post-race interview that day, and I had a bunch of people asking about my story. Jerry told me he overheard a girl tell her boyfriend that I was a total badass. I turned to Jerry and said, "Jerry, we're doing more of these!"

Jerry has since told me that he asked me to do that race to challenge me. Putting on the leader hat one more time, Jerry wanted me to see that despite my injury and depression, I was capable of so much more than I knew. And I accepted his challenge because I needed to prove something to Jerry. I needed to show him that I had come out the other side and was fine. I also think he needed to see that I was fine. So there was much more going on that day than just two buddies spending a Saturday running a race.

When I got back home I changed my workout regimen. I was no longer focused on just getting big. I wanted to build endurance and speed. I had a new goal. I was going to run as many of these races as I could.

That's exactly what I did. I kept running these obstacle races, each one building on the one before. I ran 3.2 miles and then 5 miles and then 8 miles. Steadily, I was improving. I was getting stronger, faster, better than before. I set my sights on running a Tough Mudder. Tough Mudder events are twelve miles and are much more challenging than the races I had run so far.

I called up my buddy Max. He'd served in another platoon but was with me during that first deployment in 2003. He and his brother were already experienced in Tough Mudders and they said they would go with me wherever, whenever. I said all right, let's go to Austin, Texas. Max said they were in. He also talked to Ashley Voss, the medic who stayed with me the night I was injured. Ashley now lived in Texas and said she wanted to race with us, too. I would tackle this race flanked by some serious support.

I started reading article after article about the Tough Mudder and I read a lot about injured veterans who came out to these events. But what I read was that these vets weren't finishing the races. They were out there to raise awareness and money for various organizations, but they weren't running and completing the course. I thought, *How hard can it be?* This motivated me. I had something to prove.

Now, my running leg, because of the shape of my stump, is wider at the bottom. I have a socket at the end so it holds on to the rest of the leg with the help of suction. It's made of carbon fiber and wraps around my stump. At the bottom there is a valve that allows air out but not in. As I ran the course over obstacles, I started to notice you could hear me making a faint *Psssh Psssh Psssh* sound.

As we got closer to the end of the course we came to a giant mud pit. To get through this, you had to drag yourself in and out of water, over mounds of mud, and back down again into a muddy pool of water. I came out of one of these pools and realized that my valve had broken off. There was a silver-dollar-sized hole in my socket. There was suddenly very little suction and my leg was dangerously close to sliding out. I was pissed.

"We only have three miles left. I am not coming off this course," I said through clenched teeth. I was so close to the end I couldn't quit now. Ashley ran off to find a medic and they came back with a small piece of plastic we tried to use to rig a plug for the hole. I just needed a little more suction to hold my leg on, but the MacGyver fix didn't work very well.

"Screw it, let's just keep moving. I think I can run."

As I ran my muscles were firing, blood was pumping into the muscles, and they were expanding. My muscles in my residual limb, in my stump, were expanding just enough to hold my leg in place. I gritted my teeth through those last three miles and we finished the race. I had accomplished yet another goal. I had conquered the Tough Mudder.

I kept racing and it wasn't long before I got a call from Quest Nutrition, a nutrition bar maker. All this time, Eric had paid every entry fee for every race I'd run. He'd kept his word. But Quest Nutrition said, "If you want to run a race in another state, we'll fly you there. Anywhere you want to go to race, we'll take care of it."

I ran my races in a kilt and I'd had BioTech Limb and Brace's logo on it from the beginning to show my appreciation for Eric's selfless actions. He never asked for anything in return from me, but I thought it was the least I could do. Now I added Quest Nutrition's logo because they were paying for my transportation. I wasn't paying a thing to do these races. I thought, maybe, just maybe I could make something of this fledgling professional athlete status.

My social media audience was growing. Other racers were watching me closely. One day, on a whim, I posted that I was going to run a marathon. I didn't really put a lot of thought behind the Facebook post, but as we all know now, if it's on social media, it's serious. Two days later I got a message on Facebook from a girl I'd never met.

"Are you serious about running a marathon?" she asked.

"Yeah, I'll do a marathon someday," I said, still thinking in vague, far-off terms.

"Well, next weekend I am running a race in Boston. If I complete it, I'm guaranteed to be able to buy a spot in the Marine Corps Marathon. It sells out really quickly. I've already looked into it and contacted them. They said that I can give my guaranteed slot to you and I want you to have it," she replied.

"Wow! You do not have to do that," I told her, but she replied, "I can't go to the marathon anyway. I'm not able to make that date. So it's yours if you want it."

I was so touched by this stranger's gesture, but then it dawned on me. *I actually have to run a marathon!* I hadn't been training to run, and could maybe run a mile, not even running the entire time. But I was committed.

About three weeks before the marathon, I decided that I should probably start running. I don't like to run, so I had been working out, but not actually running. I went to a state park and I ran a 5K, or 3.2-mile, trail run. It was not pretty. Later that week I did it again. I ran my longest training run the weekend before the marathon. I clocked five miles on a treadmill. As I stepped off the machine I thought, *Well, I've either got it or I don't*. And so I headed to Washington, D.C.

Someone told me before the marathon that I would feed off the crowd. I thought that sounded like a load of bull. But I was wrong. That's totally what happened. I forgot I was running a marathon. In fact, that's exactly what my friends said when they saw pictures of me. They said it didn't look like I was running a marathon at all. I was smiling, high-fiving, and chatting with the massive crowd lined up all along the way.

We had one woman on our team who was struggling a bit. She told us all to go ahead of her, but I said no, we're a team, we run this as a team. We slowed down, because she needed to walk every now and again. But my running leg doesn't walk so well, so I fell. No big deal. A little later on, maybe twelve miles in, she needed to walk again. We walked with her. I fell again and I could tell my body was seizing up. At mile fifteen I fell for a third time. I knew I couldn't fall again. I had to adjust in a different way for her. The next time she slowed to a walk I kept running but I ran back and forth across the street. I never stopped running but I was moving at her pace. If I fell again my muscles would seize up too much to continue. My fix worked, and I was having fun.

We got to about mile twenty-five, with just over one mile left to go, and suddenly I had a spurt of energy and my pace picked up. I was moving! I was passing people and trucking along. One of my friends, Mandy, said, "Noah, slow down. Calm down." Obviously I wasn't listening and I just took off. After a quarter of a mile at that speed I suddenly realized maybe Mandy was right. I was not feeling so great. I was severely dehydrated and was crashing. I slowed down. And then all of a sudden I heard a guy on the sideline shout, "Hey! I know you! You do those Tough Mudders!" I turned and saw a guy waving, with a backpack and an American flag draped around his shoulders. I smiled and said, "Yeah!" Then he shouted, "Want a beer?" He handed me a warm beer out of his backpack and I cracked it open right there and chugged it. Mandy caught up to me and, exasperated, asked, "What are you doing?"

"I don't know. He gave me a beer. It's got carbs and calories in it. I think I can use it right now. Let's go!" I took off running, before I had to slow down again. Mandy again came up behind me and asked, "How do you feel now?" She smiled as she asked me.

"Well, I don't really feel so good right now and I am pretty sure that I am drunk," I replied.

We limped toward the finish line, but before we could cross it, there was one very steep hill to climb. I pushed up it and mustered all of my energy to cross that finish line like a rock star. The crowd roared! They put medals around our necks and we took celebratory pictures. I was once again basking in the euphoria of accomplishing a goal that not so long ago, I would have believed impossible.

After we finished we were famished. "I want pizza," I said enthusiastically. We found a pizza place and no sooner had we walked in than I realized I had to get to a toilet fast. And we're talking a nanosecond of this becoming an emergency. I felt the cramping start and a cold sweat developing on my neck. I asked the woman at the counter where the restroom was and she pointed out the door. We were in an outdoor mall and I guess there was just one public restroom for all to use. I followed the direction she was pointing in and I saw a massive line to get into the restroom. My eyes must have gotten huge with panic because the manager grabbed my arm and said, "Hey, come here." She walked me around the counter and led me to the employees-only bathroom. I all but hurled my body down on that toilet seat, barely making it in time. And then I passed out. Sound asleep on the toilet. Lights-out. When I came to, I had no idea how long I'd been in there. I do know however, that my right leg was completely numb. When I finally returned to my group, they all had puzzled looks on their faces. "What were you doing in there?" one of them asked. "Pretty sure I fell asleep," I answered. "Where's my pizza?" My pizza was cold but I ate every bit of it.

With each race I did, I gained more of a following on social media. I posted pictures and updates from these races and so did other people who were racing alongside me. I was getting messages from people all over the country.

One such message came via Facebook from a woman named Ilene Boyar. She wrote to tell me how inspired she was watching me run these races. She has brittle bone disease. She used to have to rely on a wheelchair, but now she had crutches. She's broken every bone in her body at least once but she likes to hike a lot. She said, "I would love to do a Tough Mudder but I can't because I can't run." She went on to tell me more of her story, but that one line struck a chord with me. I wrote back and told her how impressed I was that despite her illness she continued to push herself. Then I told her that if she really wanted to do a Tough Mudder I would do one with her. We would walk the whole thing. She replied, "Are you serious?" I told her yes, I was. Why not?

We set our goal for a Tough Mudder in Sarasota, Florida. I reached out to BioTech and to Quest Nutrition and they agreed to sponsor a team. I then turned to Facebook and asked people who wanted to do a Tough Mudder for free. As people responded I sent out a note saying, "We're not running this race. We're going to walk it." My buddy Billy Findeiss, from Birmingham, agreed to come with me, but the rest of our team were strangers who wanted to be a part of helping Ilene.

We all met up in a rented house in Florida, a mighty pack of twelve, to help Ilene through her first race. We walked the entire course. It took us ten hours to complete but no one complained. We were all there for Ilene. On the last obstacle she showed us exactly why we had spent those ten hours on that course.

The last obstacle is called Electric Shock Therapy. There are dozens and dozens of wires dangling from a structure over a precarious pit of mud and each wire is live. Electricity shoots through the wires and if you hit one, it zings you pretty good. Most run through it so as to minimize the shock factor. Ilene couldn't run. And she couldn't very well take her metal crutches through the wires. After a brief moment contemplating her plan of attack, she handed off her crutches to a teammate and got down on her hands and knees. She crawled under the wires and I walked with her. The wires zapped me left and right but I didn't care. I was so proud of her. She could have just opted out of that obstacle but she didn't. She had come to this race with the intention of participating and finishing it. She wasn't going to skip an obstacle. She reached the other side, pulled herself up out of the mud, and grabbed her crutches. Together we crossed the finish line.

When you finish a Tough Mudder you are rewarded with a headband instead of the traditional medal. I grabbed one and put it around Ilene's brow. I told her how proud of her I was and choked back tears. That was a huge moment not only for Ilene, but for me as well. Once again I was seeing how I was still able to help people. I might not be a soldier anymore, but I had not lost the ability to make a difference for others.

After that, Ilene continued to race. She was officially hooked. She has walked through these obstacle courses one after another after another. Now she too is inspiring other people to push through their fears and their "I can'ts." Just the way I want to do, Ilene taught others what is possible when you focus on the positive.

———

CHAPTER 18

Operation Proper Exit

I RECEIVED a phone call in May 2010 from another injured veteran I'd met at an event some two years earlier. He told me he was calling from Iraq. He was on a trip sponsored by the Troops First Foundation, participating in a program called Operation Proper Exit.

When injured soldiers leave the battleground it's not always at the end of a tour. Many of us are unconscious when we are medically evacuated. This program gives us the chance to go back and leave on our own terms, and our own two feet. The hope is that we can find the closure that so many of us were denied.

The soldier said the group was doing a few more trips that year and he suggested that I be one of the participants. He hated to put me on the spot, but he had to know right then. He was in Iraq, after all. I couldn't think about it and call him back. I also couldn't talk to Tracy about it before I said yes.

Tracy was less than thrilled when she got home from work that night and I said, "Guess what? I'm going to Iraq in two months." She was upset about it, but I was already committed, and she didn't fight it. I got my passport updated and they issued me a few uniforms. I was ready for ten days back in-country.

We flew on a commercial flight to Kuwait before boarding a military plane for Baghdad. On the way I couldn't help but feel excited. I knew it wasn't going to be the same. I was no longer an infantry soldier. But I felt that maybe, just maybe, I'd get a little bit of that feeling back. Of course, I knew that was unlikely. We would not be taken anywhere remotely dangerous. They weren't going to let anything happen to a bunch of wounded veterans. We would not see combat. That wasn't really the point. So I also prepared myself for how different it would be.

When we arrived in Baghdad we were taken to our hotel. It was the same hotel that all of the celebrities stayed in when they came to entertain the troops. The hotel was run by National Guardsmen and was very safe. There was Internet access and phones to call home. There was even a pool. The camp was built around one of Saddam's former palaces. I hadn't had the luxury of living in a camp like this when I was deployed. I was front-line combat. I was living wherever we found shelter in the danger zones. But on this trip I stayed in various camps that had all been Saddam's palaces, which felt more than a little odd. Each day we flew on helicopters to the area where each of the ten of us had been injured. This was the main focus of this program. They took each soldier back to the point of injury, to give us closure. Other than those flights, we were in the camps that had once been palaces. I couldn't believe how nice they were or how well taken care of the troops were who were stationed here.

On our first flight out, and for all the following ones, we boarded two Black Hawk helicopters. On that first flight, we were looking for the area where a marine in our group lost both of his hands. While we were airborne, the door was kept open. There were only a few pairs of headsets for the group, so whoever was the focus of the trip got first dibs on a pair and would help guide the pilot to the right spot. The rest of us shared the remaining few sets as we squinted against the wind to the terrain below. Right before we made it to this marine's area, the guy sitting next to me handed me the headset. Just as I put it over my ears, I saw the marine looking out the window, and then I heard him say, "And that's where my hands are."

Suddenly it wasn't about me, the injured guy. I was privy to this man's intimate struggle. It was a painfully shocking statement. I knew all of the rest of these guys were injured, too, but I don't think it really hit me until that moment that these guys all faced the same kinds of struggles and confusion I'd faced.

One of the days we were there, the program leaders, or mentors, as they were called, told us we couldn't go on any flights because of the threat of sandstorms. To kill time, the marine who had lost his hands and I decided to take advantage of the amenities in camp. So we headed to the pool. He wasn't wearing his prosthetic hands and when we arrived, I sat down on the edge of the pool, dangled my right leg in the water, and took off my left leg. We joked about how these guys got to go swimming on their days off. I mean, days off? I certainly never had one. As the two of us removed our limbs to get in the water, we noticed one of the active-duty guys already in the pool looking at us. He did a double take before asking, "What are y'all doing here?" Without a moment's hesitation, we both said in unison, "We're on vacation." We said it with a blatantly arrogant tone as if to say, *You think you're deployed. We think you're on vacation.*

Finally, my day arrived, and we loaded up to head to my area. Since it was my day, I was seated where I could see best out of the open door and guide the pilot. I'd watched these other guys go through the emotions of revisiting the spot that changed their lives and I was ready. *Excited* is the wrong word, but I definitely felt a form of anxious anticipation. I put the headset over my ears, ready to communicate with the pilot. Just as I had the set adjusted and the volume turned up, I heard someone tell the pilot, "You are not flying into that area. That's just not going to happen. It's too dangerous."

My heart sank. I was so deflated. Everyone got to do the fly-over except me. I wasn't getting that chance at closure because even now, years later, the area was still not contained or controlled. I was devastated not only because I couldn't revisit that place, but because so many lives and limbs had been sacrificed without any victory to show for it.

After the failed attempt to return to my location, they took us to the military hospital in Baghdad. This was the hospital we had all passed through immediately after being injured. I have no recollection of being there, but I know I was before they sent me to Germany.

When we arrived they led us into a room to meet privately with some of the nurses and doctors. They lined us all up in chairs and we went down the line introducing ourselves. I was the last one in the line. When it was my turn, suddenly I was overcome with emotion. I was too choked up to even say my name. I stood up but could only muster, "I can't talk." And I sat back down. I don't know where it was coming from, but my emotions were powerful and paralyzing. Everyone carried on with the question-and-answer session and I just sat there taking deep breaths, trying to regain my composure. Finally, after I was sure my voice was steady and my tears were dry, I stood up and said that I'd like to speak.

"I don't remember coming through here, but I haven't felt this emotional anywhere else. I know none of you were here when I came through or when these other guys came through, but you're doing the same job. You're doing it for other guys here now and I just want to say thank you for what you do, what you have to see day in and day out, not knowing how things go afterwards. I hope that with our being here, you're able to see that we do move on. We do recover. And I wanted to say thank you."

I barely made it through the last few words before I choked up again. Tears streamed steadily down my cheeks. I looked around and everyone else was crying, too. Every guy in our group as well as every doctor and nurse. It was emotional for all of us.

As soldiers we all have jobs to do—whether it was out in combat or back at these combat hospitals. No one really stops to talk about what we feel inside. That moment with the medical team was the most emotional part of that trip for me. Being there triggered something deep within my consciousness. I knew that this was the closest I was going to get to thanking the doctors and nurses who saved my life that night. I was overcome with gratitude for the work that field doctors and nurses do for all injured soldiers.

Although I did leave feeling disappointed that we were unable to revisit my point of injury, I got a lot from the program. I enjoyed talking to the active-duty troops as well as the other men on the trip with me. But I wanted more. It was like being so close and yet so far from my old life. I was teased with who I once was.

After I returned to Alabama, I had a minor setback in my progress out of depression. I sat around and did nothing for about a week. I was able to shake it off and get back to the gym pretty quickly, but for a while it was really hard to be faced with that life again and not be able to resume it.

*   *   *

Three years later Troops First called me again and asked me to be a mentor on a trip to Afghanistan. I'd never been there, so I wanted to see it for myself. I said yes without hesitating.

We flew around each day to the different areas where these men had been injured. I enjoyed speaking to both the troops stationed in Afghanistan and the guys on this trip. Everything was safe and once again we never got anywhere near combat. There was one day where we were going somewhere that required us to be in an armored van. It had big bulletproof windows on the side and the seats faced each other. Everywhere we went we had a member of the infantry with us for protection and I was seated opposite one of these guys in the van. As we began to roll out, with Humvees in front of and behind us, I looked over at him.

"Hey, man, will you switch seats with me?" I asked. He said sure and we swapped. I sat down with my left side on the outer part of the vehicle, closest to the windows. He looked at me with a puzzled expression and asked, "Why did you want to switch seats?"

I answered very nonchalantly, "Oh, well, if I get blown up again, I'd rather it be on the same side. I don't want to lose my right arm, too."

His eyes opened wide. I don't think he'd ever even considered that he might get blown up. And he was probably shocked I was so nonchalant about such a catastrophic possibility. That wasn't happening in his unit. I was coming at it from a very practical place, so I said it completely calmly. But I could tell I freaked out this guy.

The worst thing that happened on that trip had nothing to do with the war or any sort of danger. It was actually at the first little camp we flew into, on the first day. When we stepped off the Black Hawks there was a sign posted with a screaming eagles insignia on it. The 101st was here. Not just the 101st, but my battalion. And not just my battalion but Bravo Company. My company.

I went right up to some of the troops and introduced myself, explaining that I, too, was Bravo Company. I stood and chatted with them for a while but then they had to go out on a mission. I walked out with them and stood and watched as they prepped and left. It was incredibly depressing to watch them go. I could no longer contribute to the team. As much as I'd improved, accepted things, and found new joys in life, it was still very hard to see the things I'd given up right in front of me again. That's not quite accurate. Giving up implies a choice. I was watching what was taken away from me and I had no control over it. Wearing the uniform again but not being there as a soldier was demoralizing.

The same thing happened when I came home as after the first trip. I sat around for another week wallowing in my depression. The thing about being a soldier was, it was a risky job. Not only could many people not cut it, but most people wouldn't even try. Some people are meant to be soldiers and I was one of those. And those trips reopened the wound of being denied the chance ever again to be one of the few who were meant to be soldiers. But the second time around, it was easier to come out of the funk. I was no longer in that place where I didn't care if I died. Once I entered my thirties, I was much more aware of life being more about my three kids than it was about me. I couldn't afford not to care anymore.

PART THREE
RENEWAL

—

CHAPTER 19

Getting Attention in a Good Way

BEING A FATHER is an incredible experience. It's the most important part of who I am. It's a rewarding role with so many gifts, one of which is getting to see the world again for the first time through your child's eyes. There is nothing like it. That's what I was thinking about as I sat next to my eldest boy on the plane ride to D.C. He had just turned seven years old and I watched him as we headed back to a place that had become so familiar to me in my recovery. This was his first flight. I thought about how I'd never even been on a plane until I was jumping out of one in basic training. My children were already getting to experience things I never saw as a kid. Even through my injury and struggle to regain my life, my focus has always been on being able to give my kids more than I had. As we descended I smiled to myself as I watched him look around the plane and out the window at the monuments that dot the horizon in our nation's capital.

People always say you shouldn't discuss politics or religion. At least that's what they say in the South. So this is not a political story. It's just an anecdote from a patriotic American. My status as an injured veteran has afforded me many great opportunities—once-in-a-lifetime adventures. One such moment came my way in January 2012. That year members of Congress made a bipartisan decision to invite veterans to the State of the Union address. I was incredibly humbled and honored when I received a call from the office of Congressman Spencer Bachus III of Alabama inviting me to be his guest. I decided to take Colston with me. I try to have special one-on-one time with each of my children as much as I can and on this occasion, it seemed fitting that my oldest should come with me.

When we arrived at Reagan National Airport there was a car waiting for us that whisked us off to the Capitol to meet Congressman Bachus. After shaking hands and a few minutes of small talk, the congressman told us he'd arranged for a private tour of the monuments on the National Mall. Now, I'd seen the monuments many times before. It was one of my regular escapes from Walter Reed during my extended stay there. But I'd never experienced them quite like this. Having a private tour and a guide was like experiencing these national treasures in a brand-new way. I learned so much more about the history of each one. Being only seven, Colston wasn't fully absorbing all of this history, and I think the day wasn't as exciting for him as it was for me, but we were still enjoying a nice day outside together. But man, did we wear ourselves out. We walked and walked and walked. At the end of our day there was just enough time to get back to the hotel and get changed for the main event.

After I got both Colston and me into our suits, back we went to the Capitol and to Congressman Bachus's office. His assistant told me that Colston would stay in the office with the staff, most of whom looked like fresh-faced interns, and then I was led down the grand hall to another room to meet up with the congressman. There we took pictures together, chatted awhile, and mingled with the other honored veterans who had also been invited in this bipartisan effort to show gratitude to those who've served. I looked around the room in amazement. I've watched the coverage of the State of the Union on the news countless times. From coverage that you see on TV of political events, you'd think that everyone hates everyone else. I've always felt like it looked like there was no respect across party lines. But being there in that room with other veterans and members of both political parties, I could see that everyone was talking to each other. There was respect. They were laughing and sharing stories and shaking hands. Behind that closed door I caught a glimpse of what these men and women are really like. They have their beliefs but they still respect the work of the other side.

Following our private reception, we were led to our seats. I was sitting in the gallery above the main floor, just to the left of the podium. Again, I was in awe. I do not discuss my political views but this wasn't about that at all. I was there, in this place that is a major symbol of American democracy, and I was watching, in real life, all of these famous men and women who serve our nation, just like I did, but in an entirely different way. The honor of being in that room was not lost on me. I wish everyone could see it the way that I did. And just as I'd seen in the private party, hands were extended across the aisle—literally—in warm greetings. It was so clear to me then just how hard these folks work to make our country even better than it already is. I gained so much respect for the members of Congress and other elected officials. It's easy to sit at home and judge based on the party you vote for, but to be there in person and witness the respect they show for one another is an entirely different experience.

Then a hush fell over the crowd, and everyone settled into their seats. This is an event filled with specific protocol, just as many ceremonies I'd witnessed in the army. As the conversations halted and the mummers fell silent, the sergeant at arms's voice bellowed, "Mr. Speaker, the President of the United States!"

The double doors at the back of the room opened and I saw him. President Barack Obama entered the room to a standing ovation. He made his way down the aisle of blue carpet, shaking hands all along the way. He finally made his way up the steps to his post, turned and shook the hands of Vice President Joe Biden and then–Speaker of the House John Boehner before turning and holding his hands up to motion for us to sit down.

"Thank you. Please be seated. Mr. Speaker, Mr. Vice President, members of Congress, distinguished guests, and fellow Americans," the president said.

His voice echoed in that grand hall and the hairs on the back of my neck stood up as goose bumps ran up my arms. I honestly cannot imagine how someone could go to an event like the State of the Union address, regardless of who the president is, and not be in awe of what they were experiencing. This was a part of history. I was present for a part of American history. This is how President Obama opened his speech:

Last month, I went to Andrews Air Force Base and welcomed home some of our last troops to serve in Iraq. Together, we offered a final, proud salute to the colors under which more than a million of our fellow citizens fought—and several thousand gave their lives. We gather tonight knowing that this generation of heroes has made the United States safer and more respected around the world. For the first time in nine years, there are no Americans fighting in Iraq. For the first time in two decades, Osama bin Laden is not a threat to this country. Most of al-Qaeda's top lieutenants have been defeated. The Taliban's momentum has been broken, and some troops in Afghanistan have begun to come home. These achievements are a testament to the courage, selflessness, and teamwork of America's armed forces. At a time when too many of our institutions have let us down, they exceed all expectations. They're not consumed with personal ambition. They don't obsess over their differences. They focus on the mission at hand. They work together. Imagine what we could accomplish if we followed their example.

It was incredible, exhilarating and it really moved me. Being an injured veteran, I am often asked if my injury made me less patriotic or cynical. Absolutely not. I am every bit as proud to be an American and proud that I stood and fought for my country as I was on 9/11, when I made the choice to do so.

That being said, we'd had a really long day. I'd run several races right before we made this trip and Colston and I had walked around all of those monuments. I was exhausted. My stump really hurt and I was sore. Being in the audience of the State of the Union is not a passive experience. Every few minutes when the president completed a thought, everyone stood up to clap. Stand up. Sit down. Stand up. Sit down. The sound of the springs in the aged chairs of the House Chamber became a secondary soundtrack. I was distracted by my discomfort and began to dread the end of his sentences. But then I noticed that not every person stood up every single time. I realized they only stood up when he said something their side agreed with. I decided that no matter what he said next, I was going to stay seated. I was really hurting. I was going to sit one round out. Well, as soon as I'd made my mind up that I was staying put, President Obama made a statement and everyone stood up. Everyone. Not half of the room. Every person in the room except me. It happened far too fast for me to correct my mistake. What did he say? "We need equal pay for women." And I just sat there like a jerk. If the president himself had looked up and to the left, he'd have seen me just sitting there, seemingly opposed to equal pay for women! Good grief! I was not seated next to the first lady, thankfully. I made sure to stand up the rest of the time.

When the speech concluded it was very late. One of Congressman Bachus's aides took me back to the office to get Colston. We opened the door and those interns looked whooped. Ties were off, hair was all messed up, and my son was running around the room energetically asking to play another game. He was bouncing off the walls and his babysitters looked like they'd been hit by a truck. I thanked them all and we headed out. A car took us back to our hotel and Colston crashed. I was able to get him out of his suit and into the bed. I was so tired but I knew I wanted to pack things up and be organized in the morning. We had just enough time to visit the Smithsonian's National Museum of Natural History before our flight home. Colston wasn't quite old enough to appreciate the private tour of the monuments or the fact that he spent an evening in a congressman's office. Maybe someday he'll look back on it and understand how special that day was. But for now, I just wanted to give my son one super-fun experience in Washington, D.C., before we left. He loved the museum. Even though I was completely worn out, it was all worth it.

* * *

I started my public speaking career before I was injured, in my sister Jennifer's second-grade classroom. As a teacher, Jennifer thought her students would really enjoy getting to meet a real soldier. I was pretty intimidated, even if my audience was a captive one full of seven-year-olds. But a few minutes in and I was at ease as I told the children all about basic training and becoming a soldier. I could do this. No sweat. The idea of public speaking didn't really come up again until after my injury and my introduction to the Lakeshore Foundation.

The folks at Lakeshore asked for my help and participation in their new programs at special camps geared to help other veterans just like me. They first asked me to talk at events in the community to raise awareness about these special camps, to help grow the program. I would share a little bit of my story and talk about the camps and how important they were and the difference they made.

Soon Lakeshore had me out speaking everywhere from Rotary clubs to black-tie affairs. I was gaining confidence and finding my footing in the world of public speaking. I was talking to groups of veterans as well. I was talking about my experiences and how I'd found fitness to help me over bumps on the road to life after combat.

I realized that maybe there was something to this motivational speaking business and that I could now pursue it as a profession. I was talking to guys just like me who'd been through the same things I had. And it wasn't like I was this extraordinary guy, it was that my injuries came before theirs. Maybe showing them the route I took would help them through whatever they were dealing with.

When I started doing these talks I was still battling depression myself. I wasn't quite practicing what I was preaching yet, but you know what they say: fake it till you make it. And I think in some way, speaking to others helped me finally find my right path.

Along with the speaking, I kept racing. I was doing every race I could find. I even started to run races with a group who wore gas masks through the entire race to raise awareness for other veterans in need. People can see my injuries. They know I was wounded and what I've sacrificed for my country. But so many men and women come home from war damaged in ways we can't see. Wearing those gas masks raises awareness for injured veterans of all kinds. That has been and always will be a priority for me.

The racing challenged me and energized me in a way I hadn't felt since before I was injured. I also started to realize, after Quest Nutrition started paying for me to compete in these races, that this could turn into something professionally. I told Eric that my new goal was to keep running races and be sponsored by a big-name company or companies. I thought I might become a professional athlete of sorts and make a living through sponsorships.

In running those races, I was getting noticed in a positive way. People weren't gawking and staring at me because I was disabled. People were cheering for me because of what I was able to do. That was a huge accomplishment. And with each race I ran, the audience grew.

I'd garnered a pretty solid following on social media and it just kept growing. And after that first Warrior Dash I had my first post-race interview for *Obstacle Course Racing* magazine. More publications like that followed and even a few local news stations profiled me. And then something happened I couldn't have predicted and certainly didn't see coming.

By this time I was pretty used to being invited to special events and contacted by various organizations wishing to honor veterans. It was all very nice and I usually tried to attend when my schedule allowed. One of these invitations came from Brad Keselowski's Checkered Flag Foundation (BKCFF).

The NASCAR driver aimed to honor veterans and their families in the way only a NASCAR superstar could. He invited us along with our families to a VIP weekend at the track and then stayed an extra day after the race to give us each a ride-along in his car. Keselowski's foundation partnered with local VAs across the country in various towns near NASCAR tracks. The staff at the VA would then nominate a dozen or so men and women who they felt either really deserved a special treat or really needed a morale boost. I was chosen by the staff at the Birmingham VA as an honoree at the BKCFF event at Talladega Superspeedway in 2012. I thought it would be a really fun thing to experience with Colston. Jack and Rian were too young then for that kind of thing, but Colston was a huge NASCAR fan.

We pulled up to the track on race day and Colston was incredibly excited. There was such a buzz around the track and the smell of outdoor grilling filled the air. Flags of every color, displaying every driver's number, flapped in the wind. If you're going to experience NASCAR, this is the place to do it.

The BKCFF folks, Andrea, Dan, and Brad's sister, Dawn, were running the show and they brought us to a VIP air-conditioned suite. It was a sticky hot day in May and it had rained early in the morning, so I was glad we were inside the suite. There was everything we'd need—food, beers, collectable cars for the kids, and even a FanVision device at each of our seats. Those allow you to listen to the different drivers' radios as they talk to their crews as well as watch the action on a small television screen. We were right at the start/finish line, but this way we could also watch the TV broadcast and know what was going on.

Colston loved it. He sat in his front-row seat and didn't move during the entire race. Brad even won that day, which was exciting. The entire suite erupted in cheers and we all got to go to Victory Lane, where the race winner receives the trophy, with Brad and his No. 2 crew.

The next day was more relaxed. It was really cool to be where fans almost never get to go, but we were also the only people who were there that day. Brad arrived and said hello to all of us and then explained what was going to happen. We would all get to have a turn riding shotgun with Brad for a few laps. There was also another driver, Parker Kligerman, who was going to take our family members for a ride. They told us Colston was too little, but Brad came over to me and said he'd figure something out. So one by one we all got to hop in the car. It's an actual race car, but this one had a passenger seat. As we waited around, we all started talking. It's always a moving experience to get to talk to other injured veterans and hear their stories. There is an immediate camaraderie there. But it wasn't just our families and us. There was a producer and a cameraman from CNN there as well. They were doing a story on Brad's foundation. The producer's name was Rebecca Baer. I enjoyed talking with her. She was very nice, but both she and her cameraman, Rich, were very respectful and kept the attention and focus on the veterans. After each of the veterans had their ride we were told to head inside to the media center for lunch. But as we turned to go someone grabbed me and said, "Take Colston over to Brad really quickly." Brad then scooped Colston up and put him in the car as he brought it into the garage. It wasn't safe to give him a ride on the track because he was too little for the safety belts. But a slow cruise just a few feet into a garage stall was thrill enough for my boy. I was touched at the extra attention he received.

We all settled in for a lunch in the media center, which was a small, square concrete building in the middle of the infield, near the pit road. On race day this place would be packed full of journalists covering the race. But that day it was just our little group having lunch. I noticed that Brad made a point of coming around to talk to all of us. And then Rebecca from CNN came around and asked me if I'd mind doing a quick interview on camera about my experience that day. I told her sure, that I'd come over to her when we were done eating.

I finished my meal, and as I tended to do, I put a wad of dip in my lower lip. A few minutes later I reported to Rebecca as I'd promised. The first thing out of her mouth was, "You're going to take that dip out first. I won't put you on CNN with dip in your mouth." I was taken aback by her bluntness but at the same time I thought it was pretty funny. I laughed and said, "Well, I just put it in." She replied, "All right, enjoy it for a few minutes, then toss it and come back to me." I laughed again. This woman was no-nonsense, but she wasn't rude about it. She had a job to do. I did as she asked and we walked into the other room to do our interview. She asked me a few questions about my experience over the weekend and what it means for people like Brad to show this kind of compassion to veterans.

When we were done, we rejoined the others, and Brad sat down to autograph various items for all of us. After Colston and I got our hats signed, I hung back and talked to Rebecca some more. She asked a bit about my story. She seemed genuinely interested and not like she was just asking or looking for a story. I genuinely enjoyed talking to her and telling her my story. It didn't cross my mind to pitch to her that she should do a story on me. After I told her the basics of what happened to me and where I was now, she turned and looked me straight in the eyes. She seemed moved and said, "Wow, Noah, that's a pretty incredible story."

I just thought that was a huge compliment; I wasn't thinking anything beyond that and I don't think she was either at that point.

She'd been working in news for a national network for a long time. I knew that meant she'd heard a lot of stories. I felt very humbled that mine impressed her. We talked a bit more and exchanged information. We kept in touch, but it wasn't until months later that she told me she indeed wanted to do a story on me.

Rebecca was working on a new project for CNN called *Welcome Home*. It was a series focused on the realities my generation of veterans faced after serving in Iraq and Afghanistan. She came to Alabama twice. I didn't really think it was a big deal because I had never been the subject of a national media story before. And by this point I was very comfortable with Rebecca. She interviewed me first at the gym where I was working out at the time, and she and her crew filmed my workout. On the second day she and her crew came to interview both Tracy and me. She wanted to capture us at home and talk more about how my injuries affected my family life. I was impressed with Rebecca's interview style as well as her professionalism. And it was only when the piece aired that I realized what a big deal that was. It was a whole different level of exposure for me.

Every time there was a story about me in the press from those racing magazines or local news, my social media following increased. After the CNN piece aired, it spiked. That really helped bolster the following I was working hard to create. I still wasn't quite sure how, but I knew that my increasing celebrity could be something. I believed I could motivate and help others and provide for my family. This was all building into something that could be really huge, I believed.

But that wasn't the only thing that happened during that CNN story. Like I said, Rebecca came to see me with my family.

She built a lot of her story around how Tracy's love pulled me through my days at Walter Reed. And how my children pulled me from the depths of my depression. Tracy and I were both very candid with Rebecca during the interview. We shared a lot, and hopefully when our story aired on CNN, it was helpful to others. But that day when Tracy and I talked so openly was our last good day.

CHAPTER 20

The Bottom Falls
Out—Again

BY THE FALL of 2012 my life seemed as if it couldn't get any
better. I felt hopeful and excited about my future. I was running
races, making friends all over the country in racing communities,
and I had a pretty steady and growing fan base. It seemed as if
I'd finally gotten control over my life again. When I was in the
deepest trough of my depression I thought there was nothing I
could do. Everything seemed over. My military career was over.
I couldn't be physically active anymore. I had no idea how I'd
come back from that. But over time, I did. I became physically
active again and then I realized I could have a new career. I realized that people who struggle with a successful past and then lose
it have to learn to accept the new normal. I am very proud of my
military service. I am thankful for it. But it was only one chapter in my life. Every chapter eventually ends. While mine ended
before I thought it would and not how I wanted, it was time to
accept that the chapter was over and move on. Once I processed

that, I was happier. Too many people end their story there. Too many people think their lives are defined by just one chapter. I enjoy talking about my military service and I am proud to have served, but it does not define me. I had finally figured all of this out and was making great strides forward.

Only back home, my marriage was crumbling. I headed out to races every couple of weekends and Tracy wasn't a part of any of it. We had drifted apart. Tracy was still struggling with postpartum depression; she'd never fully recovered from it after Jack's birth. It got worse after Rian, and between that and my neglect, Tracy had a battle she couldn't win.

She didn't deal with it head-on. She did what I had done. She tried to ignore it. She went out with her friends a lot. We functioned on completely different schedules. I didn't drink very much and went to bed early. We were ships in the night, not loving spouses. I was completely obsessed with fitness and races. When I was home my focus was one hundred percent on the kids, but not on Tracy. We started to fight over everything. Marriage is supposed to be a coming together as one but Tracy and I were now two people who just happened to live in the same house.

The kids were spending more and more time at Tracy's mom's house and this made me angry. That was just one of the many things we fought about. But they needed to be there. I never worried that the kids were in danger, but Tracy was drinking a lot and not dealing with her depression in a productive way. I couldn't judge her for that. I had done the same. But I had come out of my depression, and tried to help her, but nothing I tried seemed to pull her out. That includes what had worked for me, fitness and healthy eating, but I realize now that fitness may not have been the answer for her.

By the end of 2012 I knew that our marriage was totally broken and we would both be healthier apart. Separation would be a healthier environment for our children, too. I told her we needed to get divorced. It was an emotional discussion, but we both knew it was true. We weren't even interested in each other at this point. Still, it was an incredibly difficult reality for us to swallow. We agreed to wait until after the holidays and on January 1 she moved in with her mom. This turned out to be the best thing for her and the kids, because Tracy's mom helped her through the depression and to get a handle on her drinking. Tracy then got her own apartment and she's been fine since. I was and continue to be proud of her for making it through such a difficult period and becoming the mother I knew she wanted to be.

But my troubles were bigger than just a failed marriage. One day I asked Tracy for the password for our bank account. She'd handled much of our finances and I needed to take over that task. As soon as I asked, Tracy bristled and snapped, "That's my bank account. You don't need it."

My reaction was, "No it's not. The only money going into it is mine. I started the account, so what makes you think it's yours?"

We argued for a while before she broke down and confessed to me that she had not been responsible with our finances. In the worst days of her depression she'd failed to pay the mortgage for six months. I called the mortgage company to explain to them that I had had no idea this was happening. I had money. I could send a large amount of what I owed right then. I was told it was too late. I fought and fought, but the company wouldn't relent at all.

I called back and said, "Listen, I am putting money aside to make the payments. I've got the cash but you keep hitting me with these late fees every month." The man seemed to be receptive and said that with the amount I was able to send now, we could work through the rest. He was going to send me paperwork to sign. I sighed with relief.

I shouldn't have. When he sent the forms I read through them and realized he'd tacked on several additional late fees and several thousand dollars for unidentified reasons. The new amount we owed was far beyond what I could cover. I called back extremely angry and ended up hanging up on the guy. I felt as though I were falling backward into a familiar dark hole. I couldn't see a way out. I had another failed marriage, I owed thousands of dollars, and as the final indignity my car's motor blew out. The car I was still making payments on was now useless. I was fighting with Tracy, the mortgage company, and myself. After putting myself back together, building myself up, and finally feeling good again, it felt as though everything was collapsing in on top of me. I couldn't breathe.

It wasn't long before a letter arrived in the mail saying I had ten days to get out of my house. I'd lost the house. There was no more negotiating. I called my parents and my close friend Billy. Billy came over and helped me load everything into a truck and take it to a storage facility. It took forever with just the two of us, but we did it. We fit my entire house into a tiny storage unit. I give all the credit to Billy. He must have been a Tetris champion in a former life. When we finished my mom called.

"Why didn't you call more friends to help you?" she asked.

"Mom, this is not something I really want to announce to everyone. I don't want to have to tell people that I lost my home. The home I put thirty-five thousand dollars down on and have been paying off for seven years," I said.

I was ashamed and frustrated to be homeless and knew I was teetering on the edge of really regressing. Thankfully, I have family who could and would help. My sister let me move in with her until I was able to get an apartment. I hated that for my kids. They deserved to have a real home. Their parents were divorced but they still deserved the best I could give them.

Then I remembered a group I'd worked with to help another veteran, Homes for Our Troops. I'd helped them a few years earlier build a house for a veteran in need. They had said they wanted to build me a house, too, but I had declined thankfully. I had a home then. There were others who were in need of their services. But now I was faced with a very different reality. I found myself in a place where I indeed needed them. I reached out and they immediately agreed to help. But building a home takes time. I would have to wait a while before I was back in a real house with my kids.

All of this drama could have sent me tumbling back down the hole I'd worked so hard to climb out of. However, just when I needed it the most, hope reentered the picture.

CHAPTER 21

The Girl on
the Radio

I SAW HER as soon as I pulled into the parking lot. This beautiful woman with a gigantic smile on her face was just about bouncing up and down despite the orthopedic boot she had on her foot as she waved me into a parking space. I felt like I'd been hit in the gut. She took my breath away. She was dressed in workout clothes, her long brown hair softly framing her face, and she just glowed. I composed myself and got out of the car. She was standing with Paul Orr, the radio host I was there to meet. Local press had become fairly routine for me at this point, so I hadn't really given it much thought when I agreed to be a guest on the afternoon drive-time show for WZZK. But I had no idea I'd meet her.

Paul reached out his hand and introduced himself. And without waiting to be introduced she whipped out her hand and said, "Hi! I'm Jamie Boyd!" And right away she was talking a mile a minute. She was so chipper I couldn't help but smile. I was like that little dog in *Looney Toons* who is always following the big bulldog around shouting, "What are we going to do today, Spike?" She was adorable. She started firing off questions, one of which really caught my attention.

"So you were in the Army? What was your MOS?" she asked.

Now, *MOS* is a military term most civilians have never heard. It stands for Military Occupational Specialty. It's basically military code for "job." So instead of just asking me what my job was in the Army, she knew enough to specifically ask me what my MOS was. I was impressed.

"Eleven Bravo. Were you in?" I replied.

"Nope! But I've thought about it. I still think one day I will join the Army."

We followed Paul inside and as he set things up and got ready for his show, Jamie and I talked nonstop. She, too, was really into fitness. She was dressed and ready for the gym and told me she was about to leave to get in a quick workout before her shift on-air.

"Yeah, I have the shift after Paul Orr. The seven-to-midnight show. I call it the *Jammin' with Jamie Show*. People call in and I'll ask them if they're cryin', laughin', lovin', or leavin'."

I couldn't believe how into this girl I was, and we'd only been talking for twenty minutes. I was also dressed in gym clothes, because I'd been to the gym earlier. She looked down and saw the rubber bracelet around my wrist.

"Is that an 'I Am Second' bracelet? I have one of those!" she said as she held up her wrist with the band that means, "I am second after Jesus."

"No, this is my own bracelet with my motto, 'Train like a Machine,' on it. Just my little self-motivator. I have some in my car. I'd love to give you one."

"Well, actually, I am about to leave. I have to go work out before my shift," she reminded me.

"You can have this one. Take it off my wrist. This one will be worth more someday because I've been sweating in it," I joked.

She laughed and took it off my wrist. We kept chatting and she told me she had wanted to do an obstacle course race for a long time. Then Paul interrupted our conversation and gently reminded Jamie he had a show to do. He and I needed to start our interview. She laughed some more and smiled her way out the door.

Paul and I sat down and started the live talk. People were calling in and thanking me for my service, asking questions about my racing, all the usual topics I now regularly discussed on local news and radio shows. And then we got a call from one of my former neighbors. He still lived in the neighborhood I was forced to leave.

"Noah, those of us in the neighborhood, we knew you were going through a lot. It was obvious. But you've turned that around and we've seen that. And I just want to tell you how proud we are of where you're at in your life now," the man said.

I was floored by the unexpected but genuine expression of kindness. I turned and looked at Paul and leaned into the mic as I said, "I went through a lot of depression, and it means a lot that you brought that up because I worked really hard to get to where I am now. For you to say that you and others are proud of me really means a lot to me."

After we finished the interview Paul thanked me for my time and told me he thought I was great on the radio. He suggested I think about it as a career. I thanked him and said I'd consider it. But really all I was thinking about was Jamie. As soon as I got in my car I looked on my phone and saw I had a Facebook friend request from her. I felt schoolgirl giddy. I accepted the request and immediately called my Army buddy Max. Max is one of the guys who came with me on that first Tough Mudder. We are really close friends, and he's someone I've always confided in. Just a few weeks before I had called and told him, "You know what? I'm done with women for the time being, but the next time I talk to a girl, I'm shooting out of my league." So now I called Max and said, "I've met a girl way out of my league and I'm gonna take a shot."

I wasn't good at asking women out and felt really nervous. I told Max she had sent me a friend request and he urged me to send her a private message on Facebook.

I typed out a pretty long message and hit SEND. Then I finally put the keys in the ignition and left the radio station parking lot. Every red light I hit, I checked my phone to see if she had responded. She hadn't. Why wasn't she responding? Finally, I pulled over and looked again. The message hadn't gone through! I panicked and called Max back.

"What am I gonna do? What if I send another one and the first one is just floating through the Internet and it eventually goes through? Do I send another one? Do I make it sound exactly the same? I'm gonna look like a crazy person! What do I do? I don't know what to do!"

Max calmed me down again and I rewrote my original message. This time she responded.

"Jamie, it was great meeting you and Paul today. Sorry you got stuck with a used bracelet. If I run into you again I will hook you up with a new one. You'll just have to give that one back. They aren't free. LOL. Take care."

She responded: "Ha ha. Actually, Noah Galloway, I got the one I wanted ;). Great to meet you, too. Love your story. Tragedy to triumph. I can't imagine the number of people you inspire every day. Hope to run into you sooner rather than later."

I wrote back, "I've got an extra 50% off code for a Spartan Race that's in Georgia this coming March. Just four or five miles with obstacles. Good warm-up to a Tough Mudder. If you're interested, I gave away all the free ones already, but I have two of the half-offs. I've got one guy I'm waiting to hear back from but if he doesn't want it I will have two for you, if you want them. But definitely one. Let me know if you want one."

She said, "Yes, I am definitely interested. Can I do it by myself or do I have to be on a team? Appreciate it."

"You can do it by yourself. Not fun at all that way. You are more than welcome to do it with me and my friends. It's just four of us. Your call. Let me know."

She said, "Yes. If you don't mind I think I'd like that. Just because I'm not sure any of my friends would be down to do it on short notice. Definitely a good warm-up to Tough Mudder and I bet going it alone wouldn't be so great. Ha ha. In Conyers Georgia, looks like a two-day? Or do you just have the option to go Saturday or Sunday? Either way I'm down."

I replied, "We're going to do the Saturday run. We're probably going to hang around Saturday night. You have to work Friday night, right? I will hash out the plan and get back to you."

Then I told her how to sign up, gave her the code, and said, "I got you two if you want to invite your boyfriend or another friend to come with you as well. Same code gets you 50% off each. Y'all are more than welcome to hang out with us."

I thought that was a slick way to find out if she was single. It worked. She replied, "Sounds good, I'll try to take off for Georgia that Friday night, maybe Saturday morning depending on race time and probably just stay through Saturday night as well. I think it would be awesome to hang out with you. Great to see you have two 50% off discounts also. I no longer have a boyfriend but I do have friends. So I will see if any are available. The code won't expire in the next few weeks will it? Just so I have time to reach out to my peeps."

I told her that we were all going to stay the night on Saturday if she wanted to stay with us. We were getting a few rooms for the whole group and just crashing, so there would be a place for her to stay without it being inappropriate.

Finally I said, "Well, if you're going to hang out with my friends and me, I think we should get together for lunch, so I can find out if you're crazy. I don't want you to embarrass me." She told me she loved that idea and we made a plan for lunch.

We met at a Chipotle on a dreary rainy day. I bought her lunch and we sat down and started talking. It was as if the whole world around us disappeared. I remember a couple of times glancing over to the table next to us and seeing a couple sitting there. We kept talking and I would glance over again and there would be a different couple seated next to us. We must have spent a couple of hours in that restaurant until finally we got up to leave. We walked out, and standing in the parking lot I said, "All right, so let's get together again for lunch one day." She laughed and said she would like that, and I went in for a hug. When we pulled away she said, "You're very huggable. Give me another hug." I hugged her again and we went our separate ways.

Lunch with Jamie became a weekly event for several weeks. During that time I learned she liked the show *The Walking Dead*. So finally I got up the nerve to try to move beyond lunch.

"Every Sunday night I go to a friend's house and a group of us watch *The Walking Dead*. You should come over this Sunday." I already knew she had Sunday nights off from the radio station, so I thought this was a great plan. But she hesitated before finally saying, "I don't know. That sounds like a date. And I am a few episodes behind." I told her, "You haven't missed anything. Nothing that important." I was lying. She'd missed a lot of stuff. But she finally agreed.

She came over, met my friends, and we watched the show. Afterward, we went to grab a bite of dinner. Just like at lunch, we talked forever. We shut that restaurant down. They actually had to tell us to leave because they were closing. So then we stood in the parking lot talking. It was freezing but neither of us wanted to go home. We stood out there so long that the employees of the restaurant had already cleaned up and left. We were completely alone in the lot.

Then she did the most adorable thing. I don't know how the conversation had gone this way but flat feet came up. So all of a sudden she chirped, "I have really flat feet. I'm like a rabbit!" And then, without warning, she whipped off one of her cowboy boots and tapped her foot on the ground really fast. *Bump-bump-bump-bump.* "I'm like Thumper from *Bambi*!" she exclaimed. I couldn't believe it. I thought, *This girl is crazy and I absolutely love it.* I was laughing, she was laughing, and I decided to go in for the kiss. I leaned in and then she suddenly leaned back. Crap. I was so embarrassed.

"I'm sorry. I went in for it, and it wasn't good." I hung my head down.

"No, no, no, I panicked! Please, try again!" she said.

"No, I won't make a fool of myself twice in one night. We'll try again another day," I said and I changed the subject. I was talking about something else for a while and then she whispered, "Just kiss me." I did and it was incredible. Every moment I spent with this girl, I fell more and more in love with her.

*   *   *

We started spending a lot of time together. We did the Spartan Race together and that's what really started the relationship. We knew by the end of that trip that we were a great couple. With her late schedule at the radio station and the fact that I was pretty much just working out and training for races, living off my VA benefits and medical retirement along with some part-time work at the gym, we were able to do a lot together. We went out for meals, worked out together, and got along very well. Everywhere we went, everyone we met thought we'd been together for years. All of those weeks spent just having lunch and talking had provided a really good base for a relationship. We had such similar personalities. We were both outgoing, enjoyed being around people, and liked doing things together. She'd often say things like, "You're trouble, but I like you."

After several months of dating, I felt I was ready to introduce her to the kids. As a dad, I am very protective and cautious about that. Relationships can come and go. My kids won't meet somebody just to have that person disappear. When I felt ready I asked her if she'd like to meet my kids. She said yes and I could tell she was both excited and nervous.

She came over on a Sunday afternoon when I had all three kids with me. We went to the park and played. She's like a big kid herself, so she was a natural with my children. We came back to the house and played board games until it was almost bedtime. Jamie went home and I put the kids to bed. She came back the next day and the boys were thrilled. They took to her immediately. But Rian was harder to please and not going to give in so easily. She may be the baby but she's always known how to play it cool.

Jamie was sitting at the kitchen table when Rian sauntered up to her and said, with a bit of an attitude, "What's your name again?" Now, what's really interesting is that not even an hour earlier Rian had asked if Jamie was coming over again. So she knew Jamie's name. She was letting Jamie know that she was the princess of the house and Jamie had not yet earned her place. It took a little while for Rian to warm up to Jamie. She'd have fun with her but wouldn't get too close. But she came around. Jamie loved to wear long, colorful socks when she worked out, and Rian started pulling her socks up as high as she could and saying, "Look! I look like Jamie."

As Jamie and I got more serious, there was some friction. I criticized her for having unrealistic standards for men, and we argued. She loved movies and especially romantic movies. Her favorites were *The Count of Monte Cristo, Beauty and the Beast,* and *The Notebook,* which I also loved. But I would say to her, "Life is not a movie! That's not how real life works. Those movies are designed to entertain people. They have a pattern all of them follow and life does not work that way."

This became a real area of contention for us but it was only later that I recognized her high standards taught me how to be a better man. No matter how frustrated I got with her, I knew that if I didn't live up to her, as I called them, unrealistic expectations, I was going to lose her. So without realizing it, I improved as a person to keep her happy.

We'd been together a year and a half, but there was so much conflict, largely because of our strong personalities and how similar we were, that we decided to break up. It was hard on both of us, but Jamie also wasn't working at the radio station anymore. So without me and without her job, she decided to get out of town. She took a job at a gym in Nashville but she never rented an apartment. She moved into an extended-stay hotel. We didn't talk for weeks after her move, but slowly the calls and texts started again. We found our way back to each other slowly. She came down to Birmingham every weekend to see me. She'd stay the weekend and then leave at 2:30 a.m. on Mondays to make it back to Nashville for her shift.

Jamie used the time away from me to do some soul-searching. She finally also did something she'd thought about for a long time. She walked into an Army recruitment office in Nashville and joined the military. She didn't discuss it with me beforehand. Instead she called and said, "I'm joining the Army. It's active duty and I'm going to be a truck driver with an airborne contract." Shocked, I blurted out, "You're going to do what? No you're not."

"What do you mean? I'm gonna be a truck driver in a convoy." I knew she was referring to a seventies country song she likes. Only this wasn't a country song, this was real life.

"Are you crazy? This is not a game. You will hate being a truck driver. You don't even know if you'll like being in the military. Go National Guard or Reserves and see if you like it."

"They said I'm already in. Basic is not for another few months but I'm in and I can't change it."

"Yes you can. You are not in yet. You are not in the military. That was just a recruiter telling you that. Why aren't you going in as an officer? You have a degree. You can make more money."

She seemed annoyed that I was raining on her parade, but I think it was also dawning on her that maybe I was right and she hadn't done the research.

"They told me that it's not really that much more."

I explained to her, "They are lying to you. It is a lot more."

I had no problem with her joining the military. If that's what she wanted to do, I supported it. But I was going to make sure she made the smartest moves she could make if that was in fact what she wanted to do with her life. I certainly wasn't going to let her be talked into a lower-paid, higher-risk job.

On my next weekend without the kids I went to Nashville to visit her. We had a great weekend. On Monday morning she kissed me goodbye and left for work. I would drive home while she was at work. Only I didn't go straight home. I went and paid her recruiting officer a little visit. I walked in wearing shorts and a T-shirt so my injuries were fully visible. The two recruiters couldn't hide the surprise on their faces. I clearly looked like an injured veteran. Not their typical visitor.

"I'm here about Jamie Boyd," I said.

One of the recruiters stood up and said, "Yes, I'm working with Jamie Boyd. How can I help you?"

I walked to the center of the room between him and the female recruiter who was still seated at her desk and said, "Jamie

Boyd is not going to be active duty. She is not going to be a truck driver. She wants to change her MOS and you're not going to treat her like some high school student. She has a degree. She is a young professional and you will treat her as such."

"Yes, sir, yes, sir. We hold ourselves to a higher standard. We'll do better. I'm sorry," he stammered.

"You convinced her she can't change anything. That's a lie. It's paperwork. Make it happen."

"Yes, sir, yes, sir."

That afternoon Jamie had an appointment at the recruitment center anyway for more paperwork. Afterward, she called me, and as soon as I answered, without even a hello, she said, "What have you done?"

"How were they acting?" I asked, sounding really pleased with myself.

"Like I can have whatever I want," she answered.

"You're welcome. Find a better job." She wasn't mad about it. She just laughed and said, "You're crazy."

"I will always protect you. You were getting screwed over. And I'm sorry you didn't know about it, but you wouldn't have let me go if I had told you ahead of time.

"You're right, but I'm glad you did."

Jamie ended up choosing MP, military police, as her MOS because they offered her a huge signing bonus. We made our reunion official and she quit her job in Nashville to move back to Birmingham. She had a while before basic training, so she moved back in with me. We were both very happy, and as it turned out, some very big changes were about to happen beyond basic training.

CHAPTER 22

Stumbling into the Limelight

THE CNN PIECE aired in 2012 and brought a big boost in my social media followers, but then the numbers evened out again. I didn't give it much thought. I just kept doing what I was doing. My name was out there and I hoped I was motivating others, but I was busy living my life. In fact, I was so busy I almost missed my next opportunity.

Almost a year after the CNN piece aired, I had a voice mail from a producer at MTV asking if I would be a part of an episode of *True Life* called "I'm doing a Tough Mudder." I thought that sounded cool, but I forgot to call back, and let a couple of days go by without returning the call. Jordan Ross, the MTV producer, called again.

"I've been trying to get a hold of you to ask you about being on an episode of *True Life*," he said. I apologized for not returning the call and said that I'd love to do the show. We hit it off immediately and were joking with each other.

"Who doesn't call right back to be on TV?" Jordan kidded me.

Up to this point I'd run Tough Mudders and all kinds of races but I hadn't run one alone. So I took this opportunity to challenge myself even further and try one solo.

The filming of the show was pretty intense. MTV had a crew come down to Birmingham and film everything I did all week leading up to the race. I'd never experienced anything like that. It was a reality TV show, where cameras capture every move. They were in my house, they were at the gym, and everywhere I went. Again I saw a boost in my social media following, and more people would approach me and say, "You're that guy who runs the races in a kilt."

I fully admit to loving attention. Even though I didn't plan my celebrity, I felt all along that the point of it was to share my story and hopefully help others. I didn't go out seeking media attention but I was pleased when it came my way. I thought I could turn the racing into something profitable that could support my family. I kept telling my friends and family, "I'm working on something that could be important for me." That's why I did so many.

Well, as I finally figured out in the summer of 2013, that plan wasn't sustainable. My body just couldn't take it. My ankle was swollen constantly, I had a painful rotator cuff, and my body in general was breaking down. I decided I was taking the summer off.

I originally got in shape to be a better father. But now I was doing all of these races, killing my body, and realized if I kept going at that pace, I would not be able to do anything with my kids. So I only did one race that summer. I raced with a group of women who'd asked me to come with them to a Tough Mudder. They'd never done one and were inspired by me. And I didn't even complete that race. I skipped some of the obstacles. But that was okay. I was there to support this group of women through it. I didn't have anything to prove. I knew then that I was done with races. I didn't want to do them anymore and needed to find the next thing.

I spent the rest of the summer playing Mr. Mom. I pretty much had the children full-time. The kids had my full attention. I even had a calendar on the kitchen counter with a schedule of all the restaurants in town where the kids could eat for free. This was crucial because I don't cook. I was scheduling all of their activities and playing summer camp director. That made me laugh because it's similar to how I spent my summers as a kid. Because my parents worked, my oldest sister, Jennifer, was in charge of Sara, Katherine, and me. She called it Camp Jennifer. As a teenager she was saddled with three kids all the time but she mostly took it in stride. She took us to the pool at the community center most days, but there was always something else she had planned, too. I tried to fill these days for my kids the way she had done for us. I joked with my friends that I was doing so much with the kids my estrogen levels had risen. I was starting to get emotional during commercials. But the truth is, I loved it. It was another step in the right direction of building an even tighter bond with my three children.

A few months later I got a call from a close friend, Jeff Bloch.

"I was reading in *Men's Health* that they're going to do a search for a regular guy to put on the cover," Jeff said.

He went on to tell me that *Men's Health* usually only had celebrities on their cover, but they were teaming up with Kenneth Cole to do this "Ultimate Guy Search," and Jeff thought I should enter. During my Army days I used to tell the guys that I'd be on the cover of *Men's Health* someday. Back then it was a real pie-in-the-sky dream, but I thought about it a lot. I even thought about it again after I was injured and started to design my own workouts. I thought I had a legit story for them. But of course it wasn't a reality until Jeff's call.

I went online and filled out my application, wrote a short summary of my story, submitted my pictures, and shared my entry on social media as instructed. This was how people voted for you to win. I was going to go to bed but instead I kept refreshing the page. The one post I did was shared a thousand times, five thousand, ten thousand, and by the end of the first night, twenty thousand times. When I woke up the next morning, of the thirteen hundred people who'd entered the contest, I was already in the top three. And that's where I stayed.

The rules stated that the online fan voting only made up 10 percent of the decision. There was a team at *Men's Health* narrowing the pool and making the final decisions. I was told later that Bill Phillips, the editor in chief of *Men's Health,* told his staff that they would read every single story from all thirteen hundred applicants. He didn't care if a story only got one vote. Everyone would be considered.

I made it into the top ten and then the final three. That's when things got really exciting. The magazine flew us all to New York City for a photo shoot. Besides getting to meet with some pretty big people at *Men's Health*, this was when I finally got to meet the competition—Kavan Lake and Finny Akers. They are both really nice guys, and my first impression was that both of them, well over six feet, looked like models. I knew I might be in trouble. But we all hung out, got along, and went to a workout arranged by the *Men's Health* team, led by their trainer, David Jack. David was incredibly motivating. I felt really good after the workout, so I was feeling a little less nervous about the photo shoot. At least I did before Kavan and Finny took their shirts off. They were both so fit and handled the photo shoot so well, I was nervous. I'd never done anything like this on a national scale. There were people every-where and I was feeling really insecure when my turn came, but everyone was encouraging and with their help I got through it.

When we left, we were told it would be another month before the winner was announced. Then I felt really discouraged. Friends were telling me that my injuries and my fitness level guaranteed me the cover. I felt the opposite. I didn't feel I was as fit as the others and I felt like the war was too controversial a topic for the magazine to want to feature a wounded veteran.

I had completely talked myself out of even the slightest possi-bility of winning by the time I was back on a plane to New York a month later to find out the results. My family didn't believe that I didn't know already. They thought I'd been told and kept ask-ing me about it. But I really didn't know. The winner was being announced live on NBC's *Today* show. I had made my peace with not winning and Jamie and I were just excited to go to New York and be on *Today*. We had a layover in Charlotte, North Caro-lina, and when we landed there I had a voice mail from my friend

Billy. His message: "I thought we had to wait to see who won? It's already out!"

I clicked onto my Facebook app and saw that Billy had posted a picture of him and some of his buddies at a truck stop in Kentucky posing with a *Men's Health* magazine—and I was on the cover! I was shocked. But even then I was convinced this wasn't real. Maybe the editors had decided to give the cover to all three of us and we each had a different region of the country. It felt incredible to see myself on the cover of that magazine but I just wasn't convinced I was the outright winner.

Jamie and I got to our hotel room late. I called my contact at *Men's Health*, Nora, and said, "I've already seen the magazine." There was a beat on the other end of the line before she flatly said, "We'll talk about it in the morning." So Jamie and I went to bed. The next morning we met up with Finny and Kavan and headed over to 30 Rockefeller Plaza for the *Today* show. I didn't say a word about what I'd seen.

When we arrived, Nora was at the door. I waited for the others to go in before I said to her, "So we're not going to talk about what we're not going to talk about?" I was smirking a little but quickly wiped the grin off my face when I saw the look on Nora's.

"You're not the only person in this competition, Noah. Not everyone knows." Roger that. I wouldn't say another word. After going through hair and makeup, we got to the set and sat down with *Today* host Matt Lauer and Bill Phillips for the live reveal. They had a blowup of the cover but the person on it was a black silhouette. Now, the silhouette did have two arms and two legs, but that could have been just to throw us off. Both Finny and

Kavan said, "I don't know, Noah, that looks like it could be you." I just said I couldn't tell.

The show took a commercial break and after the break they pulled down the silhouette to reveal that it was me. It was true; I had won. I made the cover! Finny and Kavan were going to be inside the issue, and they were fine with it. It was only then that I told them about the truck stop. They both looked at me. "You knew?" they asked. I nodded, still not quite believing it was true.

After all the excitement, Jamie and I went back to the hotel room and that's when I was hit with an immense wave of guilt. I called Finny and apologized. "Finny, I'm sorry. I'm sorry that you or Kavan didn't win the cover just because I'm an injured veteran. You deserve that cover."

He said, "Noah, you didn't win that because you are an injured veteran. You won and earned that cover because you are a tough son of a bitch. You are physically fit. The things you've come back from, the things you've experienced and overcome, that's why you deserve this cover."

He talked me off the ledge and made me feel better. But then I got off the phone and another wave of guilt crossed my mind. I thought, *How is this going to look to other injured veterans? I am going to look so cocky and arrogant on the cover of this magazine.*

But within a day or two I started getting messages on Facebook and emails from veterans and veterans' families, who reached out to me and thanked me for being a positive image of the veteran community. I did not see that coming. Only then was I fully able to celebrate and appreciate what it meant to be on the cover of that magazine.

There was a lot of buzz about the cover, and I was getting calls from all kinds of press. Before we even left New York, media outlets called to talk to me. Jamie and I were out walking through the city when we got the call I'd been hoping for from Ellen DeGeneres's show! Jamie and I love Ellen. We would DVR it and watch it late at night before we went to bed. After that call, Jamie and I were supposed to fly straight from New York to Los Angeles to be on Ellen's show. Only Ellen's team made a change in plans and delayed my appearance by a week. Jamie was leaving for basic training in just a few days, so she'd miss the chance to go with me. She was disappointed. I said, "Look, I don't know what's about to happen but I'm going to work hard while you're gone. Whatever happens is going to be bigger and better than you getting to go to Ellen." I had no clue what was going to happen next, but I just knew bigger things were coming. I would make sure of that.

CHAPTER 23

———

Long-Distance Love

(October 2013–February 2014)

WHEN JAMIE left for basic training I knew exactly what I had to do. Of course, I knew what it feels like to be in basic training. I knew the best thing I could do for her was to write her letters. A lot of letters. What's funny is that when you write a letter you can feel like you've written so much, but that same letter can take two seconds to read.

I remember getting letters when I was in basic, and I'd read them and think, "Man, that's it? I read it too fast."

Contact from back home is so crucial. It means so much. I remembered how I felt. I remembered telling Brandi, "I don't care what you say. Just ramble. Ramble about your day."

She never grasped that. It was always just this one-page letter and then it was done. So after I got Jamie's address, I wrote to her every day. Every night after I put the kids to bed, I would write. I would tell her about everything that had happened—what I did, what the kids did, something funny one of them said. I just wrote as much as I could for several pages. Every night I wrote her novels and every morning I mailed them to her.

That was all well and good until I found out I'd addressed all of the envelopes incorrectly! I'd left out one digit of the zip code on every single letter I'd written. I was devastated. Even though I had put a return address on them, I was sure they were stuck in post office limbo.

I had this realization the same day I got my first letter from Jamie. I ripped it open and read it through gripped fingers. She told me all about her first few days in basic training, and at the bottom she added the most heartbreaking line, "I wish you'd write me. I know you're busy and I know you don't like to write, but I wish you would."

I couldn't believe it. She thought I hadn't written at all.

I called a buddy of mine who is now Command Sergeant Major Phil Blaisdell, a battalion sergeant major at Fort Jackson, South Carolina. "Phil, I'm in trouble. Man, I've been sending her letters and I was putting the wrong zip code on them and I got a letter from her and she thinks I'm not sending her letters and I know she needs that."

"All right, let me call you back."

A little while later my phone rang. "I'm Command Sergeant Major Duncan. I am the battalion sergeant major of Fort Leonard Wood, Missouri. First of all, I'd like to tell you that I know who you are and I appreciate your service and what you've done. I've seen your *Men's Health* issue and you are an inspiration. I understand you know a Specialist Boyd," she said.

"Yes, Sergeant Major, I do."

"Well, I've got her standing in front of me right now. Would you like to talk to her?"

"Yes, Sergeant Major, I would." So she handed the phone to Jamie. Jamie was a little stressed out because she had been called to the sergeant major's office and thought, *What have I done?* The conversation was rushed and she was speaking in a hushed tone.

"Hey, I miss you, I love you."

"Hey, me, too, baby. Let me tell you real quick, I've been sending you letters—"

"I got them all today. Thank you."

"I miss you, and I hope that you can tell."

"Look, I want to keep talking but they're watching me."

"Okay, we're good. Just wanted to make sure you got the letters. I love you and we'll talk later."

I hung up the phone. She wasn't allowed to use the phones yet, so this was the first conversation we had had in three weeks. Every day after that I sent her a letter. After the initial three weeks she was allowed to use the phone for five minutes every Sunday. After that, it went up to ten minutes.

While she was gone, since I was already sending her letters every day, I ordered envelopes that had her address on them and little stickers that had my return address that I'd stick on the envelopes. I didn't stop there. I also ordered some stamps that were a picture of her and me. Even though I sent the letters every day, some days she would get several at a time. Each letter I wrote was several pages long, so I'd take one page and I'd glue one stick of gum in the middle and fold it up. So she could have the gum they weren't allowed. She said she would chew on it at night in bed. I had experienced enough of that world to know those little things mattered. I knew exactly what her days were like and how hard they were.

She was getting so much mail that when they called out names to pass out the mail, they'd just toss Jamie's on the ground and she'd have to pick it up. And they made fun of the envelopes with the stamps I'd had made. But she got all her mail.

She was at Fort Leonard Wood for six months—from October until March. I made sure she got tons of mail the whole time. But this also meant she would be there on Valentine's Day. I made sure that she felt loved on that day. I bought her a Valentine's Day card and enclosed a chocolate bar in that letter. The card read:

> *Jamie, we can't be together for Valentine's Day, so I came up with a way to at least show you how much you are loved. Valentine's Day is twenty-four hours long. So expect twenty-four separate packages with a card and chocolate. I'm so proud of you. Love always and forever, Noah.*

In the days leading up to Valentine's Day, in addition to the daily letter I also made sure to send her a Valentine's card and a different bar of chocolate. I was buying really nice bars of chocolate, all different flavors and kinds. She was only allowed to eat them right there at mail call, and sometimes she would get several packages at once, so even though it was hard to do, she'd share bites of her chocolate with other people. I also made sure to give extra thought to the regular, daily letter that would arrive on Valentine's Day:

Jamie,

In the beginning of our relationship I criticized your expectations in a boyfriend. I told you that you watched too many movies and lived in a fantasy world. In a way I was asking you to settle. Even through our arguments about what was realistic and what was a fairy tale, I did everything I could to be your prince in a world where I saw you as the princess that you are. I was wrong to ever question you. Your standards never dropped and it forced me to rise up to the level needed to keep you. Like a storybook romance, I've defended your honor, showered you with love, worshipped the ground you walk on, and will faithfully wait for you while you're away. You have made me a better man. Because of you I live a life I am proud of and have become the father, brother, son, and friend my family deserves. Your love has positively affected every aspect of my life. And for that I could never repay you. But I will happily be forever yours, paying off my debt and love for years to come. Like your favorite movie, Beauty and the Beast, *a tale as old as time, we are living proof that fantasy can be reality.*

Love always and forever,
Noah

I'd never been that outwardly romantic before. I'd never worn my feelings on my sleeve quite like I did with her.

CHAPTER 24

Suddenly My Dance Card Was Full

(2015)

AFTER THE *Men's Health* cover my life took a turn I couldn't have seen coming. I now had a manager and a professional team fielding calls from media outlets wanting interviews. There were also calls from executive producers calling to ask me to be on various television shows. As exciting as that was, my priority remained my children and Jamie. I even got a call about *Survivor*, which I thought was pretty cool. But I didn't think twice about turning it down once they told me how long I would have to be away from the kids and not even be able to talk to them. That was not a possibility for me no matter what the show was or how much money was on the table. I was not going to do anything that kept me away from home too long.

Then there started to be a buzz from my fans on social media about ABC's *Dancing with the Stars*. I didn't think much of it other than that the hype was funny. I'd never watched the show but I'd heard of it. But then my manager told me, "*Dancing with the Stars* wants to talk to you." I couldn't believe it, but I said sure, I'll take their call. I spoke to members of their production team, who told me they were interested in the fact that I was missing an arm. They'd never had anyone on the show who was missing an arm before. They'd had amputees on the show, but with different injuries. Mine posed a bit more of a challenge for dance. They mentioned Amy Purdy, the double amputee, who had been on the show, so I said, "Yeah, Amy Purdy is amazing, a very athletic, very impressive woman, but she has both of her knees. I don't have a knee on my left side." The phone went silent for a little while. But it didn't turn them off. They just resumed talking.

"Do you have any dance experience?"

"No."

"Anytime in your life, if you were at a bar or a club, what did you do?"

"I stood at the bar and ran my mouth. That's what I do. I have never danced in any capacity. I don't dance." I was not trying to sell myself to them at all. I was being straight with them.

Then they said, "If you decide to do it, we'll put you in a house in L.A."

I knew then I had to say no to this show. "Well, I'm sorry, I've got three kids here and I can't be away that long." And without hesitation Deena Katz, one of the executive producers, said, "That's fine. Your dancer will come to where you are and that's where you'll rehearse and come back and forth. Where do you live?"

"Alabama."

She just answered, "Okay." I don't think they thought about that, either. Alabama is a long way from Los Angeles. We talked a little while longer and that was it. I never said yes. They never said I was doing it.

Two months passed and I heard nothing. I was irritated. We'd rearranged my speaking engagements based on the time period when we thought I'd be working on the show but still heard nothing. I finally started to look around online for information about the show and I saw that they were going to announce the new cast for the twentieth season of *DWTS* on *Good Morning America* the next Monday. It was Wednesday. I thought, *Man, they could have told me I wasn't going to be on there. Don't just leave me hanging and disappear.*

I was pretty disappointed. Later that same night I got a call from my management team telling me that I had to be on a plane on Sunday to go to California to be on *Good Morning America.* I'd made the cast of *DWTS.* My response was probably not what my team was expecting. I told them I didn't know if I wanted to do it. They had waited until so late to ask me. I didn't like the feeling of someone saying, "Jump," and me having to jump. But my manager insisted that this was not something I should pass up. I mentioned that I already had two speaking engagements scheduled for that week and she said, "I'll handle it. You need to say yes to this." So I went to Los Angeles.

I arrived late on a Saturday night and Sunday morning they took me to a boxing gym to film me working out. This was also where I would meet my dance partner for the first time. I'd never seen the show, so the anticipation of who it would be was lost on me. We started filming and in walked this tiny woman wearing blue jeans, a black shirt, black boots, and a large-brimmed black hat, only half containing a wild mane of the brightest red hair I'd ever seen.

"Hi! I'm Sharna Burgess!"

One of the first things I said to her was, "I'm sorry."

"What are you sorry for?"

"Well, I know this is your job but you got stuck with a guy missing an arm and a leg."

She looked down my body and said, "Oh my God, I didn't even—honey, I didn't even notice you were missing your leg, but that's okay. We're going to work with that."

"I may be missing an arm and a leg but what I'm missing in limbs I will make up for in hard work," I assured her. I don't think she realized how much I meant it. I told her that I had three kids back home in Alabama, so I'd have to commute back and forth. She was fine with it. Then I said, "In March my girlfriend Jamie graduates from basic training. And that's in Missouri. It's very important that I go." That didn't seem to be a problem, either. Sharna was very upbeat and said, "We'll go. Wherever we have to go, the show will find us a place to rehearse."

The next morning I had to be up really early to meet the rest of the cast for the first time and get on a bus from the hotel to the *Good Morning America* set. To be honest, I didn't realize who most of the cast were yet, but I found Sharna. I'd been thinking all night about something I needed to tell her.

When we got on the bus I turned to her and said, "You're not going with me to Missouri when my girlfriend graduates from basic training. Yes, it's important for us to rehearse but Jamie is beautiful and even looks adorable in a uniform, but she doesn't feel pretty. And because she doesn't feel pretty I don't want you to meet her for the first time when she doesn't feel her best. So I will go to her graduation and come right back and then y'all can meet another time. With complete respect for my girlfriend, I'd rather it go like that." She nodded and that was the end of the discussion.

When we arrived at the studio, Sharna and I were the last to get off the bus, because we were the first on. As I stepped off the bus the first person I saw was Robert Herjavec. He walked right up to me and introduced himself. He asked if I was a veteran and I told him I was.

"My girlfriend is actually in basic training right now," I said. "She'll graduate while we're on the show." He comically threw his hands up and said, "Of course she is!"

We had a good laugh and I knew immediately that I liked this guy. The next person I saw was Suzanne Somers. She and her husband waved me over. They introduced themselves and we chatted a while until the producers came to get us. They lined us up behind the set in order of introduction. The dancers were on one side and we were all on the other. I was standing behind Rumer Willis. Right before we went on the air, I leaned forward and whispered, "Don't even think about falling." She whipped around and said, "Why would you say that?" I smiled and said, "Just don't fall while you're out there!" We both stifled our laughter and it was time to go. That set the tone for what my friendship with Rumer would be like. We busted each other's chops the whole time.

The show went live and we all filed out and sat down. The anchors started asking questions and I think they asked me what

I hoped to get out of the show. Without thinking I said, "I just want to make my kids proud." I didn't plan that answer, nor did I plan to get all choked up about it right out of the gate. It was subtle, but my voice definitely quivered a little bit. I heard someone utter under his or her breath, "Oh, shit." I didn't mean to be playing to the audience already. That was my true, from-the-heart answer.

Rehearsals started that very afternoon. However, I learned a little while later that because I was the last person they signed on the show, I had the least amount of rehearsal time for that first dance. Yes, they gave the guy missing two limbs the shortest rehearsal time. That first afternoon was just a chance to see what I could do. Turns out I have really good hip action! So at least I was starting off with a plus.

We had a week before the first show, so Sharna and I flew back to Alabama. I still had dad duties, after all. The show found us a rehearsal space, so every morning I would drive my kids to school and then meet Sharna to rehearse. She told me that our first dance would be to the song "I Lived," by OneRepublic. We listened to the song and when I heard the lyrics I was moved.

We both worked hard. I threw myself into learning how to dance. I didn't want to look like an idiot on national television. Poor Sharna had a lot to teach me. I didn't know the first thing about dance, and on top of that, traditionally the man leads. She had to teach me how to dance and then lead me but make it look like I was leading her. I was lucky to be working with someone so talented.

I went into this show thinking I wouldn't last more than the first two, maybe three weeks. But we made it past that mark.

Pretty soon Sharna wanted to try lifts. She saw that I was really strong, so she decided she wanted to try some different things in rehearsal to use later on. We couldn't use lifts yet on the show (that would come in the final weeks), but Sharna loved that I was up for trying just about anything.

One day she said, "I wonder if you could hold me up in the air with one arm?" I said, "Like lockout hold you?" And she said, "Yeah, but I don't know how I would get up there." I said, "Well, you know what a kettlebell is?"

I explained to her that it's pretty much just a weight, a ball of iron with a huge handle on it, and there is a movement called "the snatch" where you are just taking a heavy object from the floor and hoisting it overhead. "Because I do a lot of those I have an idea. I think I can lift you up there and lock you out. But you're going to have to trust me."

Because I don't have a knee on it, my left leg was no help at all. I told her, "I'm going to squat down on one leg as you come at me, and put my hand level and as close to my shoulder as I can. And I'm going to have to put my hand below your belly button, so I have more of your pelvis to distribute the weight evenly. In one movement, I will press you up." I told her I was going to have to push up straight from my shoulder.

"You're gonna have to come at me. I will put my hand out, then you're going to have to let your body go over my shoulder. And let me press you up." That took a lot of trust on her part. We took a deep breath and went for it. She came at me, I went down to one leg, and *boom*! The cameraman shouted, "Oh shit!" Our producer Alex said, "Oh my God!" It was awesome. We were going to use that at some point. But it wasn't time.

We got to the week of the show where they asked us to pick a song to dedicate to someone. Of course, I dedicated mine to Jamie. We settled on "Homegrown Honey," by Darius Rucker. I was excited, but I felt a little sad, too. Jamie was still in basic training for a little while longer so she couldn't be there for her song. She did call and tell me that they'd agreed to let her watch the show that night. Well, little did I know that that was a fib.

Sharna and I did our dance and in the post-dance segment where we get our scores, host Erin Andrews asked me about Jamie. I started to talk about how much I missed her, but then all of a sudden Erin stopped me and said, "I think you have a guest here." And there she was! Uniform and all! I was so happy and surprised. It was great to have Jamie there and be able to introduce her to everyone, including Sharna. We only got to hang out that night before she had to go back, but we were going to see each other in just a few more days. Her graduation was right around the corner.

Now, because she'd come to the show like that and already met Sharna, I felt a lot better about bringing Sharna with me to Missouri. I also realized by this point that missing that much rehearsal time would be a huge mistake. I told Sharna she could come with me. We rehearsed every free minute we had but still made sure to be fully present at graduation for Jamie. And the best part about that was, when it was over, Jamie came home to Alabama with us.

On this trip Sharna asked me about wearing a prosthetic arm. She thought it would be very helpful for our Argentine tango. I took her to meet Eric at BioTech. He showed her exactly what kind of arm would work best on me and she said she wanted me to wear one. Usually making prosthetics takes time, but Eric and his team made me that arm in forty-eight hours. That was awesome, but I was worried. I told her, "I don't wear an arm. I walk fine on a prosthetic because I wear it every day. I don't use an arm, so it's going to be weird adjusting to using it."

Deep down I knew there was no way this was going to work, because the movements I needed to use that arm I wasn't used to making. I had worn one before, but I didn't end up using it. This one was more high tech and I wasn't used to that. Flexing my muscles in my residual limb to connect with the hand motion was new. I would need weeks to become halfway decent at that. A guy who wears it all the time can do incredible stuff with one of these arms. I also had to learn how to dance.

It didn't take long in rehearsals for me to get frustrated with the arm. It stressed me out. And the more stressed I get, the more I sweated. And the more I sweated, the harder it was to keep the arm in place. At one point I threw it on the table and cursed. Of course, this was caught on camera. I felt bad about that later but it was the heat of the moment.

I pulled Sharna aside and said, "We're doing our first lift this week. I don't want to wear the arm to do it. People at home who don't understand prosthetics will think that I was only able to do the lift because of this arm." She said, "But the lift has nothing to do with the arm."

"I know that. You know that. But the people at home watching TV don't understand that." Finally she made the call that we'd do the dance without the arm. And we did well. The crowd loved it. Sharna was happy. I was critical of myself, but we made it through to another week.

We'd made it through to Most Memorable Year week. This was a big deal. Sharna choreographed a dance that really embodied my whole military experience and went through my injury. We chose the song "American Soldier," by Toby Keith. This was the week we were going to put in our secret weapon, that one-armed lift. It was the perfect time to use it.

It was all very exciting, but the truth is, I was hurting. I had strained muscles in my wrist, had to get cortisone shots, and was wrapping my body in kinesiology tape regularly. I was in a lot of pain. I decided that this was going to be it. I would do this dance and then I'd tell them I needed to go home. I was worn out, stressed out, and Jamie was back home now. I wanted to be with her and the kids. I think Sharna sensed I was losing steam. She wanted this dance to be emotional for me. She needed me to feel it to be able to make the audience feel it. Only, I didn't. I just wanted to go home. This was also the week where Sharna kicked me in the face in rehearsals and knocked a tooth out. I was pretty beat up.

So we got to the show that night, and despite the injuries and setbacks in rehearsal, we kept the showstopper lift in our routine. I just focused on the steps and that lift.

I still wasn't feeling the emotions she wanted me to feel. At least I wasn't until they played the video before we danced. It's a very emotional video and I heard myself say in it, "The worst thing I ever did was not open up to anyone during my depression."

The way the dance started was with me standing next to a mirror where you could see I looked whole. I loved that Sharna came up with that concept, because one day I just told her about how looking in the mirror made me upset. And so she loved the idea of the mirror.

When the dance begins, the mirror is there and I look complete, and then the mirror turns and I'm facing it. Then we go into the dance and I turn and then I pick her up to do a move where she goes back and then we do another move where I pick her up, spin her around into a cradle hold, and then down and then we hit the floor, we push back, we go into the star form, we come down, we rotate, we grab each other's arms, we lift each other up, we hug, and then she goes to the left, and I turn and face her.

I looked at her and nodded to say, "We got this." She ran up at me and I lifted her and locked out and when I did it, I saw the crowd jump to their feet and cheer. I was reminded in that brief moment of the wall I climbed in my first Warrior Dash. Everyone cheered and I didn't want to put Sharna down. When we finished, the crowd roared again, and in the judges' comments segment, judge Bruno Tonioli told me that I was a titan among men. I felt amazing. We didn't go home that week.

I found renewed strength that week from performing the dance, and I also started hearing from other veterans telling me how inspired they were by what I was doing. They said that by opening up about my depression, they were able to open up about theirs, to ask for help. That changed everything. Suddenly I wasn't in it to win. I was in it to make an impact each and every week that I was allowed to be on the air.

I started bringing in kids with disabilities and their families to use my tickets for the show. I paid for the plane tickets myself or through my No Excuses Charitable Fund. My kids had come week one. It was amazing to have them there cheering for me. They were so proud.

But my kids also had to go to school, so I couldn't fly them out each week. They did watch me on television every week and they would call. Colston especially took an interest and he would call or text me from his grandfather's phone. I loved how proud I was making my children. It was okay that they weren't there with me each time.

Bringing out the children with disabilities and their families became a mission for me. I was going to use my time on this show to help as many people as I could. I was hyperfocused now. I had Jamie with me out in Los Angeles, but I spent most of my free time studying the dances, the music, or the themes. This wasn't about me anymore.

I made it through long enough for the week of team competitions. This week also had an unexpected impact on me. By this point I was pretty friendly with a lot of the cast, especially Robert Herjavec. Earlier on he'd brought a friend out to the show, a sixteen-year-old cancer patient named Daniel. Robert had met Daniel through the Cancer Kiss My Cooley Foundation. Meeting Robert had been Daniel's wish. Humbled and a little perplexed as to why he'd be someone's wish, Robert was more than happy to oblige. Since that meeting, Robert had stayed close to Daniel and his family. Robert brought him to the show and Robert told me that Daniel specifically asked to meet me, of all of the people on the show. He was a wonderful kid and it was touching to see Robert with him.

At our first rehearsal for team week, Robert and I were put on the same team. That first rehearsal was mostly for the pro dancers to figure out the choreography and the themes. Robert and I knew we couldn't contribute much, so we hung back and joked around. Then someone told us that there was beer in the refrigerator in the rehearsal room. That wasn't normal, and since we were just hanging around, Robert and I each decided to go grab one. The cameras stayed on us as we came back into the studio. Everyone looked up and we said, "This dancing stuff is hard!" Everyone laughed and then the serious people got back to work.

We sat around and checked emails on our phones. After a while I heard Robert sniff a few times. I looked over and saw that his eyes were red. I asked him what was going on and he mumbled something about losing a friend. I could tell he was upset and needed some privacy. I jumped up and said, "Let's go outside." We got up to walk out of the side door of the rehearsal studio. You had to walk down three steps to the door and kind of bend down as you walked through. I almost shoved Robert through the door as I hurried my way down behind him. Only I was focused on Robert and miscalculated. I slammed my head into the door frame. *BOOM!* I stumbled backward and realized everyone had stopped and looked at me. "Are you okay?" they shouted.

"Yeah, I'm fine. We'll be right back." And I took Robert outside. He likes to smoke his cigars. I told him to smoke one and tell me what happened. I sat down on the curb next to him and just let him talk. It was Daniel. Daniel had lost his battle to cancer. Robert opened up to me and poured out his emotions. We'd already become friends but this was the moment where I saw his heart. I'd long admired and respected him for his business sense and all I could learn from him, but in that moment my admiration reached a deeper level. I knew this was a person I could look up to.

Each week brought new challenges and new experiences. I worked hard to improve each week, and I guess the audience saw that because we kept making it through. I could tell I was growing both emotionally and physically and I felt such motivation to keep going.

I had Jamie there with me. In the beginning that was great. We'd been apart for six months while she was in basic training and I'd missed her so much. And I was so proud of her. When she got to Los Angeles I sent her out with our rental car and my credit card and said, "Go find a beautiful dress to wear to the show; go get your hair done. I want you to treat yourself and feel beautiful." I felt she had earned being treated like a princess. It wasn't until later, as I looked back, that I realized she needed more attention from me, beyond the pampering. I was so focused on the show and learning the dances that I was neglecting her, even if we were in the same room. My work ethic is a singular focus. I have a really hard time balancing and multitasking when I have a goal. She'd never seen that side of me before.

When I wasn't rehearsing, I was thinking about the dance, about the song. I was listening to the music and she felt nothing from me. She went from six months away at basic training, but still feeling my love because I was sending her letters and packages every day, to being right beside me and feeling shut out. My head was on the show the entire time. This created a tension under the surface that would later become a big problem. But of course I didn't see that then. Yes, I was focused on the show, but I also still felt completely in love with her. And she was being totally supportive. She stood by while I worked and cheered every week while I danced.

Within the first week of the show I'd made a joke to Sharna and our producer Alex that if I made it to the end, to the finals, I would propose to Jamie onstage. I said it jokingly then, but the truth was I'd been looking at rings the whole time Jamie was at basic training. I knew I wanted to propose to her. And I knew I wanted to do it in a big way. So when making it to the finals started to actually look like a reality—something I never suspected when I made the comment originally—the topic of proposing on the show came up again, although first, another comment came back to haunt me.

Erin Andrews said live on-air, "Noah, you said if you made it past week five, you were going to buy a motorcycle. It's week eight. Have you bought a motorcycle?" I laughed and admitted that no, I hadn't bought the bike yet. What only a few people knew behind the scenes was, the reason I hadn't was that my money was going toward a ring. A few of the producers approached me about proposing on the show and I said that yes, I would still be okay with doing it, so they helped me set it all in motion. I was rehearsing nearly every second of the day and Jamie was around. Getting out to buy the ring was going to be difficult. Secretly the producers brought in a woman to talk to me. She opened up her laptop and said, "Hey, we're going to pick out a ring, and I am going to go out and get it for you."

Since I'd already been looking, I knew exactly what I wanted. I picked out a princess cut diamond ring. It was gorgeous. And then I gave the woman my debit card and she went to a store right there in Hollywood. She texted me a picture of the ring and the price. Without hesitation I said, "That's it!" I want to make it clear that I paid for that ring, not ABC. It was definitely a ring

I never thought I'd be able to afford, but being on the show and being paid each week I wasn't eliminated, I was making more money than I ever had before.

So they brought me the ring and our tight little secret circle planned how we would do it. It was week nine and the finals. It was down to me, Riker Lynch, and Rumer Willis. I would be dancing two dances that week, the Viennese waltz and the pasodoble. I told the producers I'd do it on Tuesday night during the reveal of who was going home, because I knew there would be more time. He said, "No, there's no time. Let's do it on Monday night." I was worried about that because I didn't want to take away from someone else's moment, someone else's dance. But we went ahead with that plan and I was going to propose right after my Viennese waltz. I thought that was a pretty good idea, since I would be in a suit for that. But I also found out that Riker was set to dance right afterward. So I pulled Riker aside before his dance.

"Riker, I'm thinking about proposing to Jamie on the show after my dance, but it's before yours and I don't want to steal any attention away from you. I don't have to do it. I can do it another time or another way." Without hesitation he said, "No, dude, that's awesome! Do it! That's fine!"

Sharna and I danced our Viennese waltz and right after we did it one of the judges, I think Carrie Ann Inaba or Julianne Hough, said, "This is the most relaxed we've ever seen you."

They were praising me for how relaxed and comfortable I was on the dance floor, which I thought was interesting because I wasn't thinking about the dance at all. All I was thinking about was that I was about to propose to Jamie. I guess it helped me during the dance.

Once offstage we went to what was called the red room, where Erin was to get our scores. This is where our secret team had everything staged. Sharna was to my right and Erin was to my left and on the other side of Erin was Jamie. Now, of course Jamie didn't know, but I did tell Jamie, earlier in the week, "Hey, go get yourself another really nice dress and get your hair and makeup done. I think they're going to interview you live on the show."

"Really?" she asked me.

"Yeah, they're just going to ask you how you think I'm doing."

It was the perfect cover. She didn't suspect a thing and she looked beautiful.

As we stood in the red room waiting for our scores, the operation was put in motion. Earlier I'd given the ring to the show's production assistant, Tracy. She discreetly handed the ring to Sharna behind her back. I was waiting for my signal. Sharna hit me on the back with the ring in her hand and I reached back and grabbed it. I turned to Jamie.

"You've been so supportive," I said, "I love you so much, Jamie, and there's no better place I'd rather do this than right here."

And I went down to one knee and asked her to marry me. She said yes and hugged me. Erin Andrews, who had no idea, said, "Oh my gosh! Jamie, did you say yes?" Jamie replied, "Oh, heck yes!"

Everyone in the room was crying and cheering. It was amazing. After the cameras stopped rolling to cut to commercial, Erin pretty much collapsed into a chair and said, "Oh my God, Noah, you could have told me! I almost cried on national television."

She thought it was sweet but was caught off guard. She got a lot of grief on social media and in the press about it, actually. People thought she rolled her eyes or looked mad. But I assure you, she was just trying not to cry. She was very happy for us.

In the end, I didn't win. I came in third and I heard from a lot of fans telling me I should have won. I thought Rumer deserved to win. She was so impressive.

I knew by week two she was going to win and I told her that. She was the real dancer. And I was happy for her. Riker came in second, and I was happy for him. He'd worked hard and deserved that, as well.

I had achieved big things on my own on that show. I accomplished things that went beyond a win. That wasn't what being on that show and staying on that show meant for me, anyway. Two of my dances both topped 40 million views on YouTube. And that was the important thing to me. Not in a vain way. I knew that I had gotten everything I needed out of that show. I learned more about myself and I showed all of those millions of people what is possible if you focus on what you can do and not what you can't. I showed my kids that. I wasn't just telling them. They could see it.

CHAPTER 25

Personal Growth and Loss

BECAUSE OF *DWTS*, every week a new group of people learned my name and heard my story. In the weeks that followed the show I got more and more requests for speaking engagements or media appearances. There was everything from presenting at the CMT Music Awards to being a special guest at a music festival to motivational speaking engagements. I was busy building a brand and a business that would help support my family. But I also made sure that my family remained the priority. I made sure if I had to go somewhere, I flew in, got to my hotel room, thought about my speech until I had to give it, and afterward got out of there as quick as I could to get back to my kids.

It was tricky because I only had Colston on the weekends. He lived farther away than Jack and Rian, so whenever I was home during the week, I tried to drive to Tuscaloosa one night a week just to have dinner with him. It was an hour-and-a-half drive each way, but I didn't care if I got home late. I just wanted to make sure my kids never felt they weren't the most important things in my life.

Jamie went everywhere with me and was a huge help. She was copied on every email and was able to help manage everything. She kept my schedule straight. And then one day I blurted out, "I don't want any more kids."

"What?" she asked, taken by surprise.

"I don't think I should have any more kids. I am working so hard to travel and spend time with the kids that I just don't think I can do it. I don't think it makes any sense."

I knew this wasn't fair. It's not like we'd never talked about it. A year before this happened, I had told her that I wouldn't mind having more kids. In fact, I told her I wouldn't mind having more kids in a stable home with a mom and dad who lived together. It would be good for Jack, Rian, and Colston to see that. They got along with Jamie and everything made sense. But then suddenly I felt I couldn't do it. And really, I was thinking about the kids. As much as I loved Jamie and as great as she was for me, I had to look at it like I look at everything else. What was best for the kids? And I didn't think having more children would be good for them. I would be spread too thin. It would take away time from the others. She tried to argue, and said, "I'll be there with the kids when you're not."

"I don't know. You want to travel. I don't see me having any more."

"Well, I don't want any right now. So we're fine."

But we weren't fine. I left it for the moment, but I knew it was only a matter of time. The unspoken tension just grew. A little while later I brought it up again.

"We're going down a dead-end road. You don't want kids right now, but we've been together for almost three years. Are we going to stay together for five more and then after eight years of being in a relationship you're going to decide 'I want kids now' and go find someone else? We went on lunch dates for almost a month before we even went on a real date. You're not the kind of person who's going to just go out and find someone else right away. You take your time."

We were at an impasse. She might have said she was okay with not having children of her own, but I knew that wasn't true. And she deserved to have kids. She would make a great mother. I didn't need to hold her back from that. But because we had a few trips already planned, including a big trip with my whole family to Disney World, which we'd planned for two years, we decided we would break up after that.

Of course, that didn't work. We went on the trip with my siblings and their families and we put on the best face we could for the kids. My focus was solely on making that trip magical for my children and my family. And we did that until the end of the week. My older nieces volunteered to babysit the kids while the adults all went out in Downtown Disney. After a few drinks, the fracture in our relationship couldn't be covered up any longer. We got into a huge fight in front of my siblings. We knew that night that it was over.

The next morning, on what was supposed to have been our last full day there, we told the kids we were going to leave early so we could drive back in two days instead of one long one. The kids were fine with it and none the wiser. I made sure we stopped overnight at a hotel with a pool, and that we stopped early enough so they could swim before bedtime.

They were so excited. It was almost laughable that we'd just had this lavish Disney vacation—even more than I planned, because once we arrived, Greg Bell, the head of talent relations for Disney in Orlando, reached out and said he'd like to set us up with a guide. He said that after *DWTS* I was too high profile to just walk around the park. I insisted a guide was unnecessary, but he insisted right back. We had all sorts of special VIP perks, like private meet-and-greets with the big guys and gals—Mickey, Minnie, Donald, Goofy—and all of the princesses. The works. The kids enjoyed every minute of it. But you'd have thought swimming in that hotel pool was the coolest thing they'd ever done. I was grateful for that, though, because Jamie and I were hurting and had to hide it.

A few days after we got back, I was scheduled to go out to Los Angeles to be in the audience of the next season of *DWTS*. Jamie was going to come with me, but now that just wasn't a good idea. Instead, while I was gone, she packed up her stuff and moved out of my house. That trip to California was hard, too, because as soon as I got to the show, everyone asked where Jamie was. She's so lovable and everyone on the show had gotten attached to her. I didn't tell anyone yet. I just said she couldn't make the trip. I didn't explain why.

When I got home, it was late at night. I walked into my room and it was painfully empty. And then I saw it. On the bed were the engagement ring and a letter. I couldn't read the letter. I still have it but have never read it. I was too sad and ashamed about hurting her.

Because I'd proposed to her on national television and now had some celebrity status, my management team said that we needed to make a statement. It could be in our own words, but Jamie and I had to make a statement announcing our breakup. We wrote it together over email and then we chose a date and time to post it. We texted each other right before we had decided we would post it, and then we each hit ENTER on our keyboards.

There's nothing more final than an official statement declaring to the world that your relationship is over. It was the hardest breakup I've ever had. And that is not a dig at Brandi or Tracy. I just think I was older, more mature, and more capable of forming a deeper connection with Jamie. And I did. I had a deeper connection to her than to anyone else I've ever known. As painful as it was to walk away from her, I know it was for the best for her and for me. And I will forever be thankful for the time I had with her. She made me a better person.

Conclusion

AS A CHILD I believed I was a superhero. I went through much of my life pretending to be invincible. I was mostly fooling myself about that. But after my injury people have often referred to me as a war hero. I am uncomfortable with that label. I didn't go on some heroic mission and valiantly save my entire unit. I was a guy who got riled up on September 11, wanted to defend his country, and joined the Army to go to war. And then I got blown up. I sacrificed for country, yes. But I'm less comfortable with applying the word *hero*.

But I do hope my story inspires people. That's why I tell it. It's not a Hollywood story. I have made a lot of mistakes. And it's taken me a few tries to right some of those wrongs. But the thing is, I keep moving forward. Every step I've taken in my life, even the missteps, have been forward. I've faced hurdles that were situations I put myself into and some that were beyond my control.

I grew up with parents who worked all the time and still we didn't have a lot of money. I didn't grow up with a lot, but I did learn the value of hard work. I learned what it meant to have a real work ethic, no matter what the job was. I don't think I was pushed in the right ways or hard enough in the failing school system I was part of. But I still found things that interested me and I still learned the value of learning any way you can. As a parent now I believe my shortcomings in school have made me better at parenting and encouraging my children to stay engaged with learning and with school. I may not have paid attention in class but I found that I was interested in fitness, so I grabbed every book, magazine article, or video I could get my hands on to learn more.

Mostly I learned how to be successful in life as myself. I spent so much time with a mask on. I hid my emotions and my depression behind that mask. I hid my insecurities behind that mask. I hid who I was. I am no longer trying to portray something or someone I am not. If I do something wrong, I apologize as quickly as possible. I've also learned that emotions are okay. All my life I felt I had to hide them, and I still don't wear them on my sleeve. I'm just cautious as to when I let them out and with whom I share them. But I am fine with expressing them. I'm not ashamed to tell you that I cry at commercials sometimes. Newsflash: real men do cry. I am teaching that to my sons as well. Too many men live with the idea that a real man does not show emotion. And if someone sees me cry, well, then that's a lesson for him.

That's another thing. I spent so much of my life chasing what it meant to be "a man." Growing up I always felt I had to prove myself as a man. Now I feel like I've done that. I was willing to go to war when my country needed it. I suffered an injury and fought through that, and then I pushed myself physically more than I ever had before—missing two limbs.

With everything that has happened, it would be really easy for me to crawl in a hole and say, "It's not fair." But I feel the opposite. A friend of mine asked me once, "If time travel were real, where would you go?" I said, "I would love to go back to when I was first in the hospital. I would go back and tell myself that everything is going to be okay. You are going to have some ups and downs, but you're going to be fine."

He looked at me and said, "If you could go back in time, why wouldn't you just go back and stop yourself from being injured?"

I said, "I hadn't thought about that. But I wouldn't do that." I wouldn't change anything that happened to me. If I had a do-over I would want to go through that depression, would want to go through everything that happened. I would want to screw up and end up spending ten days in jail. All those things had to happen for my life to come out the way it did. I wouldn't change anything.

Do I still get pissed from time to time that I have one arm and one leg? Yes, I do. Do I put on a pair of blue jeans and think, *Man, from the right side this looks amazing,* and then turn and look in the mirror and see that the left side the leg is smaller, the left butt cheek is smaller, and get pissed off? That's just pure vanity, but yes, it's there. But then I say, *You know what, that's okay because everything else is good.*

I am also asked a lot about whether or not I would let my children join the military. The answer is absolutely yes. I'm not going to push them into the military, but if they want to join, I will support them.

I was an infantry soldier. The whole point of the infantry is to seek out and destroy the enemy. This puts you in some tough, dangerous situations. There are a lot of jobs in the military that will never put you in harm's way. If my kids wanted to go into the military, learn a trade, learn a job, gain appreciation for the country, and wear the uniform, I would be very proud of that. I would share my experiences, and hope they could learn from them. I would encourage them to take advantage of all of the training and schools the military offers. I would say that was a mistake I made, not doing those things.

I am teaching my children to love their country. I still love this country and am just as proud to be American as I was before I went to war. I still believe this is the best country in the world. I absolutely hate it when people bad-mouth America. It's fine if we don't all agree over politics or policies or who we vote for as president. But disagreeing should be done with respect. Don't just sit there and tell me that this country has gone downhill. It hasn't. America is constantly moving forward. Sometimes the pace isn't as fast as we'd like, but we are going forward. I feel everyone should take a moment and have a little more appreciation for what we do have in this country and for the sacrifices others have made. I have lost brothers in arms who have given their lives for this country, and I am proud of my badge of honor, the wounds of war I will always bear. I will always be proud to be an American.

The biggest lesson I've learned in my life is one that I am still learning. And that is how to be the best father I can be. Everything I do now is about my children. In every decision I make, I first think about how it will affect them. I will never stop working on my relationship with my children and will always strive to teach them well. I am the most proud when I look at the three of them and see what good people they are. I will devote every day of my life to making sure they are cared for, and that they never lose their kind hearts.

Acknowledgments

TO THE BRAVE MEN of Bravo Company with whom I served in the Army, I want you all to know that I try every day to make you all proud and to represent you well.

I would like to thank all of the medical staff responsible for taking care of all of us throughout our deployment. Harley Shanklin, our platoon's medic, you were such an important member of our team and I am grateful to you. Also I'm thankful for the dedicated Army medics on the battlefield the night I was injured, including Captain Segui, my dear friend Ashley Voss Liebig, Jorge Morales, and many others who worked tirelessly to save my life and others. I also owe a depth of gratitude to the medical team at the hospital in Germany and the entire staff of Walter Reed National Military Medical Center.

After my return home, my medical care continued. For that I would like to express my thanks to the staff of the Birmingham VA.

Eric Eisenberg and everyone at Biotech Limb and Brace, I'd like to thank you for seeing what I was capable of post injury well before I ever saw it and pushing me towards achieving it.

Since my injury, I have worn the armor of injured veterans. I am now very aware of just how much people selflessly give of themselves to help soldiers like me who don't come home the same as they left. Thank you Lakeshore Foundation, Homes for Our Troops, Operation Enduring Warrior, America's Fund, and Troops First Foundation.

To my dear friend and platoon leader, Jerry Eidson. You are a friend for life. Thank you for challenging me to focus less on my disability and more on what I was able to do and do well. I also want to thank you for your help in the research for this book. Your memory is much stronger on the details than mine.

I found a path out of my injury and depression through challenging myself physically. With each new challenge, I had old friends there for support. Thank you Max and Sean Miller, Ashley Voss Liebig, Mandy Goff, and Billy Findeiss. Billy, not only did you run countless races with me, you're the best PR person I've never paid! And thank you Jeff Bloch for helping me keep my struggles in perspective.

I would like to thank the staff and patrons of the Alabaster YMCA, the city of Alabaster, and the state of Alabama. I'm humbled by the hometown hero status you've bestowed upon me.

I am humbled by the amount of public support I have received. Every time I am thanked for my service or congratulated for an accomplishment, I am extremely grateful and fueled to work harder to be worthy of such attention.

To Rebecca Baer, my partner in writing this book and more importantly my friend. You were the first to put my story in the national spotlight. But beyond that, I am grateful for the genuine connection we made as friends. As soon as this book became a reality, I knew that there was no one else I would want to write it with me.

On Rebecca's behalf, I would like to thank her parents, Emily and Dennis Baer, for their support of both of us throughout the duration of writing this book.

I would also like to thank Jordan Ross from MTV, the amazing people at *Men's Health* and the Ellen DeGeneres show for all for their friendship and for being such champions of my story.

To Deena Katz and her team at *Dancing with the Stars*. Thank you so much for taking a chance on this guy who was not only missing two limbs, but really couldn't dance at all. I guess you can teach an old dog new tricks.

Sharna Burgess, you are amazing. Thank you so much for putting in the time, the work, and the effort it took to put up with me for the amount of hours you had to every day during *DWTS* in order to tell my story through dance.

During my time at *DWTS*, I formed some pretty special bonds with other contestants but none stronger than the friendship I made with Robert Herjavec. Robert, thank you so much for not only becoming a close friend but for taking me under your wing and becoming a mentor in this next phase of my career.

My management team, Erin McLean, Kristin Glover, Kaleigh Tait, Rachel Mantesso and the rest of the folks at the Herjavec Group as well as my publicists Penny Vizcarra and Sara Lambley and my assistant Jennifer Campbell, you all deserve medals. Thank you for putting up with me.

I would like to thank Brandi and Tracy, my two ex-wives. Although our relationships ended, I will forever be grateful to both of you for giving me the three most important gifts in my life: our remarkable children. You both are also still very supportive of me and of my role as their father.

I would like to extend my thanks as well to all of the service men and women in uniform today and all of the generations before us who've heroically served this country. Your service is what allows us to all have what we have as Americans and for that, I thank you.

I want to bring special attention to my Uncle Johnny. He is a Vietnam War veteran and he too was injured in the line of duty. Uncle Johnny and the other veterans of his time continued their service well after their tours of duty ended. These men have improved how our veterans are cared for today. And for me personally, Uncle Johnny was there by my side from the beginning of my injury and still continues to support me today.

I would like to thank Mom, Dad, and my sisters, Jennifer, Sara and Katherine. You have all been by my side through every moment in this book and so much more. You've all shaped me into the man I am today. I love you all and I truly appreciate all you've done for me and my children.

And lastly, Colston, Jack and Rian, everything I do, I do with your best interest at heart. I put you first and I always will. There is no more humbling experience than being the father of three young children. Every day I look in the mirror and tell myself to be the best person I can be so that I can help shape and mold you all into the best people you can be. I love being your father and I love each of you.